The Costs of Default

A Twentieth Century Fund Paper

THE
COSTS OF
DEFAULT

BY ANATOLE KALETSKY

 Priority Press Publications/New York/1985

Copyright © 1985 by the Twentieth Century Fund, Inc.
Manufactured in the United States of America.
ISBN: 0-87078-159-6

Foreword

The great international debt crisis, which has made headlines over the last year or two, has receded back to the financial sections in recent months. If we are to believe financial editors and their sources, whether private bankers or government officials, the greatest threats to the existing international monetary network are now safely behind us. There were casualties (Continental Illinois, for one) and damages, of course, to bank earnings, to living standards in the debtor countries, and to the public treasuries of creditor countries, which have had to help directly with fresh loans and indirectly by adding to the resources of the International Monetary Fund (IMF) and the World Bank. But there were no major defaults and no collapse. Given the dire warnings of impending disaster that were so much in vogue when the crisis first broke, it is understandable that a self-congratulatory mood had broken out in the world's financial centers.

There is no denying that the international financial community has responded constructively to the crisis. The IMF and the World Bank have demonstrated initiative and flexibility. The central bankers who congregate at the Bank for International Settlements have done their part. So have most commercial bankers. Even the Reagan administration, whose initial reaction was to leave things to the free market, cooperated. Indeed, the resurgence of the American economy sparked a demand for imports that benefited both the developing countries and our industrialized allies.

But the rejoicing may be premature. The truth is that the debtor nations have been adding to their debt, not reducing it. Default has been staved off, but only by stratagems that have made conditions much worse in many countries. The developing countries are being forced to increase their exports and borrow more in order to service their debts. Their citizens have had to tighten their belts; investment in domestic industries has suffered; and imports have been cut to the bone. The long-term prospects for real growth, then, have worsened. If conditions do not soon ameliorate, economic distress may give way to political turmoil.

The Twentieth Century Fund has been especially interested in the political consequences of the international debt problem because it is a subject too sensitive for most governments or private institutions to discuss in public. If history is any guide to resolving the difficulties of excessive indebtedness, then the crisis is not over when the first emergency rescue efforts are put in place. They are usually successful because debtor countries fear to default and the creditors do what they can to prevent default. Most defaults take place only when the crisis is past and things begin to improve. Then, one or another debtor government, facing political pressure, decides that defaulting may be the only way to remain in power. It is this danger that still looms.

It is also a danger that Anatole Kaletsky, a correspondent with London's *Financial Times,* believes should be taken into account by creditor as well as debtor countries. In this paper for the Fund, he points out that much of the debt rescheduling now being negotiated is close to a form of default, and that it might be better to face up to various contingencies if political pressure in the debtor countries intensifies. He proposes a series of options that are intended to solidify the progress made in the past couple of years while enabling the debtor countries to resume growth much more quickly than the ad hoc measures taken to date will allow.

Kaletsky's forthright and well-reasoned approach makes a solid contribution to dealing with the problem of indebtedness. His solution is not something that debtor or creditor nations can publicly adopt. But it is something that is essential to rational contingency planning. If a real celebration on surmounting the debt crisis is to take place, Kaletsky's proposals must be heeded.

M. J. Rossant, DIRECTOR
The Twentieth Century Fund
January 1985

Contents

1
A Deceptive Calm

The fiscal history of Latin America is replete with instances of govern-mental defaults. Borrowing and default follow each other with almost perfect regularity. When payment is resumed, the past is easily forgotten and a new borrowing orgy ensues. This process started at the beginning of the past century and has continued down to the present day. It has taught us nothing.

—Max Winkler, *Foreign Bonds, an Autopsy*
(Philadelphia: R. Swain Company, 1933)

For at least five hundred years, governments and nations have regularly defaulted on their foreign debts. Recent history suggests that sovereign lending debacles have followed a fifty-year cycle of monotonous predict-ability; today's problem borrowers were among the nations which defaulted in the 1930s, the 1870s, and, in some cases, the 1820s.

Yet in the crisis of the 1980s, none of the major debtor countries has so far refused to honor its obligations. Thus bankers who feared two years ago that a default might be inevitable are now breathing easier, while in the debtor countries, the tentative signs of economic revival appear to be diffusing internal pressures for default; orderly reschedul-ings have been agreed for 1985 and even, in the case of Mexico, to the end of the decade.

The current calm, however, may be deceptive; the evidence presented in this paper suggests that the period of greatest danger still lies ahead.

The emergency measures implemented by the banks, the International Monetary Fund (IMF), and the debtor governments have been greatly facilitated by two unexpected developments: the near-record boom in the U.S. economy and the willingness of debtor governments to cut their nations' living standards farther and faster than even the most sanguine creditor had dared to hope.

But the implementation of an "adjustment program" does not mark the end of a country's debt problems. It may be only after the initial success of an *economic* adjustment, directed at the achievement of a foreign exchange surplus to the exclusion of almost every other objec-tive, that the gravest political challenges arise. Brazil and Mexico have astonished the world with their ability to swing from massive trade deficits

1

into even larger surpluses, but the cost has been deep economic depression and high inflation. In exceeding the balance of payments targets set in their IMF adjustment programs, Mexico and Brazil have impressed their creditors by checking the rise of their foreign debts. But they also have scaled back their plans for economic growth and development even more drastically than the IMF had planned.

As both the successes and the sacrifices of adjustment become more manifest, politicians in debtor countries will begin to demand rewards in terms of higher domestic consumption, price stability, jobs, and national self-determination. Huge trade surpluses—matched by the corresponding outflows of foreign exchange for debt servicing—may come to be seen as indicators of oppression by creditors, rather than as symbols of economic success. It must be questionable whether trade surpluses of $10 billion to $15 billion a year (see Tables 1.1 and 1.2)—much higher, in relation to gross national product, than those achieved by Japan, for example—can be sustained for decades on end by countries as poor and populous as Mexico or Brazil.[1] Yet such continuous surpluses lie at the heart of the current "solution" to the debt problem. This solution has simply shifted the distortions created by the borrowing and lending sprees of the 1970s from the structure of international finance to the structure of world trade. If trade surpluses should shrink in the years ahead, as a result of reflationary domestic policies, of a deteriorating international environment,[2] or of a rise in protectionism, then even the generous multiyear reschedulings agreed for Mexico and Venezuela will founder.

Setbacks which the debtors might suffer in the years ahead from developments in the world economy are unlikely to be met with further sacrifices. Internally, political priorities are moving irresistibly toward the rapid restoration of domestic growth at almost any cost. If, as is probable, external conditions begin to worsen and the world economic cycle turns downward sometime in 1985 or early 1986, the debt crisis could return in a new and acute form.[3] At that point it may become apparent that the margin for error in the present arrangements is desperately thin.

By 1985 or 1986, conditions in several of the debtor countries could make them more determined to resist the demands of their creditors. Debtor governments will not accept the expansion or prolongation of retrenchment policies. Many will have built up large reserves to cushion their economies against a period of confrontation with the world financial community. After a period of ever-growing dependency on the outside world, they will have increased their self-sufficiency in oil, food, and other vital raw materials. Above all, they will have recovered a degree of political self-confidence. Under these conditions, new and more serious threats of sovereign default could not be ruled out.

History confirms that insolvent governments sometimes become more, rather than less, daring in asserting what they regard as their national prerogatives once their economies start to improve and their nations recover from debt-induced paralysis. In the 1930s it was not until the worst of the depression was over, and the enormous difficulties of reviving rapid growth had become manifest, that Brazil, Peru, Chile, Bolivia, and other Latin-American countries followed Mexico in defaulting on their foreign debts.[4]

It is excessively complacent, therefore, to assume that a "bottoming out" of the debtor economies will be sufficient to ensure against a breakdown of the present rescheduling arrangements. To prepare a rational response for this contingency, bankers, politicians, and monetary authorities may have to abandon a number of illusions that have contributed to the current policy paralysis on international debt.

The first illusion concerns the starkness of the options which debtor countries supposedly face: either they cooperate fully with the present procedures for debt renegotiation or they turn their backs on the community of nations by flagrantly repudiating their debts. Repudiation is not the only alternative to cooperative debt rescheduling, as the variety of moratoria already employed by some of the debtors makes clear. Yet the false dichotomy between cooperative debt rescheduling and outright repudiation has led many analysts to overlook more plausible forms of default, such as the imposition of unilateral interest reductions. Such options raise issues of greater relevance than the simple refusal to honor all debts.

If debtors can select an intermediate position, amounting to what I term "conciliatory" default, which lies somewhere between cooperation with creditors and outright repudiation, the analysis of incentives and deterrents to default must become much more complex, and more clearly grounded in institutional reality. The decision on default will then depend on a delicate balancing of costs and rewards, all of which are inherently uncertain. Once the possibility of default is admitted, the relationship between bankers, debtors, and creditor country governments begins to have more in common with a game of poker than with a traditional commercial negotiation. A close look at the cards, moreover, suggests a deck which is stacked in favor of the borrowers, not the bankers.

The legal and financial deterrents to default are minimal in comparison to the potential financial gains which some debtor countries might make by reducing or evading their obligations. Truly effective sanctions against default exist, but they can only be applied by the governments of industrialized countries, not by the banks. This implies that the calculus of default will depend largely on the attitudes of creditor governments, especially, of course, the U.S. government.

Thus, in the continuing confrontation between banks and debtors, the whole debt issue will move increasingly onto the political plane. The final outcome could depend largely on a careful assessment of national interests by the U.S. government and, *mutatis mutandis,* by the governments of other nations in the industrialized world. For all these governments, the priority will be to protect their domestic economies, and the world trading system, from a collapse of the shaky structure that is international banking. If they succeed—and the evidence suggests that they should be able to do so—their next consideration will be the international political impact of their responses to default. At this point they will have to reexamine another set of illusions, concerning the role of the IMF.

So long as the current system of semivoluntary debt rescheduling survives, the IMF seems destined to play an important—in some cases, dominant—role in debtor country economies.

The growing influence of the IMF could well have a salutary effect on Third World economic management, but it carries political dangers. When a debtor nation is on the brink, political leaders may cite the IMF as an institution whose strictures should be heeded. When a debtor nation begins to recover, however, the IMF is likely to be transformed into a scourge that should be defied.

Even from a narrow institutional standpoint, the IMF and its staff do not claim to be qualified to manage developing countries' economies on a permanent basis, or to advise them on ways to improve their longer-term performance. If any institution exists to offer this kind of service, it is the World Bank.

Much more important, it is doubtful whether a permanent role for the IMF or the World Bank will be consistent with notions about national self-determination held in the debtor countries. If these international institutions acquire a lasting dominance over domestic development policies, the Third World is bound to demand something in return—much more substantial debt relief, a greater say in their management, or both. Beyond such demands for a "democratization" of the IMF and World Bank could lie the familiar calls for large-scale redistribution of income and "economic power" along the lines of the New International Economic Order.

Such a revival of Third World political militancy may be hard to imagine against the background of the current demoralization in so many developing countries. But the experience of adjustment under IMF control is reinforcing rhetoric calling for an end to dependency and economic imperialism. Perhaps the greatest danger which the debt crisis holds for the long-term interests of the United States and other industrialized countries is that the very adjustment that is strengthening the economies of many debtor countries will weaken their political and ideological bonds with the West.

There are ways to avert these dangers and to relieve the fear of impending calamity which will continue to overhang the world's financial markets until the debt problem is permanently resolved. But no solution will be feasible unless banks, creditor governments, and debtors accept that each must bear a share of the costs. To succeed in doing this, a third illusion will have to be rejected: the idea that the costs of resolving the debt crisis can be—or ought to be—shared out between bankers, debtors, and creditor governments in proportion to their share of the "blame."

This view is obviously naive, since moral righteousness has never been a determining factor in foreign policy or in international finance. It acquires importance because of its relation to another issue: the need to respect the rule of law in international economic relations. Only if it is widely acknowledged that banks and creditor governments share a responsibility for the excessive debts of the Third World, is it possible to arrive at a rational and constructive approach to the abrogation of existing loan agreements which the debtors are likely to require.

Shared responsibility is realistic, intellectually as well as politically. The borrowing and lending decisions of the late 1970s were part of a single nexus of economic and political events. It is impossible to criticize the borrowing policies of the debtor countries without deploring their economic strategies—and then questioning the political structures which these economic policies helped to sustain. In several cases, of which Chile and Brazil are only the most obvious examples, the borrowers' economic policies were actively encouraged by the United States and other creditor governments. In other countries, substantial capital inflows were an important condition of survival for pro-Western regimes whose political and economic strategies might not have met with the creditor governments' wholehearted approval, but which were considered preferable to the alternatives.[5]

The sovereign lending boom of the 1970s was also encouraged by Western governments because it served an even grander geopolitical objective: the preservation of a market-oriented noninstitutionalized system for distributing and recycling the world's financial capital after the 1973 and 1979 oil crises. Staving off demands for an international redistribution of income through official channels and for a general politicization of economic relations might have been much harder in a period when the Third World appeared to be in the ascendant, following the success of the OPEC cartel, had it not been for the recycling, which in turn was motivated by the overenthusiasm of bankers for lending, and the developing countries' erroneous belief that borrowing could be a substitute for long-term direct investment and official capital flows.[6]

It would in principle be quite possible to resolve the debt crisis permanently and securely through a cooperative restructuring of the developing countries' debts. As the final chapter of this study shows, such a fundamental solution need not be unduly expensive to taxpayers in industrial countries or ruinous to the banks. But no permanent solution is probable until the world begins to recognize the three themes outlined in this chapter—the genuine risk that a default might still occur; the fragility of the economic and political underpinnings of current adjustment programs; and the need for governments and banks to share in the burden of debt relief. Such recognition seems unlikely to arise spontaneously. It may prove impossible for bankers, debtors, and creditor country governments to be brought together without the catalyst of an actual or imminent default.

2
Political Risk in Sovereign Lending

It is sometimes thought that the usual rules of lending do not apply to sovereign borrowers. It has been said that lending to countries is less risky than lending to businesses or individuals because a country, unlike a business or an individual, will always be around. Country lending, it is said, is free of final bankruptcy and definitive loss. All that is needed is occasional rescheduling that gives the borrower a breathing space and does not significantly affect the earnings or capital of the lending banks. In my judgment, this is too complacent an attitude. . . . The past few years' experience suggests that our ability to anticipate future problems in this sphere is modest.

—Henry Wallich, governor of the Federal Reserve System,
International Conference of Banking Supervisors, 1981

"A country can never go bust" was the familiar, and comforting, refrain of bankers during the sovereign lending boom of the 1970s. Yet, far from offering maximum security to the lender, the virtual impossibility of putting a country into bankruptcy and forcibly liquidating its assets can be a fatal handicap for the lender to a sovereign state. In a sovereign loan, the creditor's ultimate line of defense—collateral and legal protection—either does not exist at all, or does not exist in a form commensurate with the amount of money at issue. A country's ability to service its debts, then, does not guarantee the creditors against loss. It is the borrowing government's *willingness* to pay—the "political" risk, as it is sometimes called—which is critical to sovereign lending arrangements. This is why, contrary to the bankers' presumption, country lending is often riskier than normal commercial banking.[1]

The special risk associated with sovereign lending was widely acknowledged in the past. Because the only real security for a sovereign loan lay in the "faith and credit" of the borrowing country, some authorities went so far as to assert that sovereign lending had no higher legal status than a simple wager. Sovereign loans, in this view, were just a form of gambling, with the outcome dependent on whether or not the foreign sovereign chose to pay.[2]

In 1877, the English court summarized its lowly opinion of sovereign lending in a famous judgment on the default of some Peruvian government bonds:

[These] so-called bonds amount to nothing more than engagements of honor, binding, so far as engagements of honor can bind, the government which issues them, but are not contracts enforceable before the ordinary tribunals of any foreign government, or even the ordinary tribunals of the country which issued them, without the consent of the government. . . . [3]

U.S. authorities could be even more scathing. The American commissioners negotiating the annexation of Cuba after the Spanish-American War in 1898 expressed the following contemptuous view of Cuba's outstanding obligations:

. . . as regards the so-called Cuban debt, the creditors, from the beginning, took the chances of the investment. The very pledge of the national credit, while it demonstrates on the one hand the national character of the debt, on the other hand proclaims the notorious risk. . . . [4]

In the last ten years, new legislation has strengthened somewhat the legal standing of creditors to sovereign nations. But the basic weakness of the sovereign loan contract remains as evident today as it was in the nineteenth century: the fate of the loan depends as much on the borrower's willingness to pay as on his ability to do so.

When lending to a sovereign nation, it is not sufficient, as bankers have found out, to project cash-flows forward for the life of the loan and determine that sufficient earnings will be available for debt-servicing. The degree of hardship that might have to be suffered in generating these earnings must also be determined. If the economic effort required by debt servicing is excessive, the political willingness can disappear.

Bargaining Power and Default

Normally, in spite of the virtual absence of effective procedures to enforce loan contracts, sovereign borrowers continue to service their debts. Their reasons for doing so can be divided into two categories: the fear of sanctions and the hope of obtaining further loans.[5]

For the first three decades after World War II, when debt and equity capital were moving at a gradual and sustainable rate from creditor to debtor countries, it was widely believed that the expectation of additional capital inflows would provide borrowers with sufficient motivation to abide by the prevailing rules.[6] Little attention was paid to sanctions because it seemed unlikely that they would ever be needed. It was always recognized, of course, that as borrowing expanded, a stage could be reached when the cost of servicing existing debts would start to exceed the new loans available from the markets. But this turning point was not expected to arrive for many years. By the time it did, bankers theorized that developing countries which had been importing capital would have grown into mature industrial economies, capable of reexporting the money they had borrowed.

The conditions of the 1970s transformed this theory beyond recognition. The combination of excessive borrowing and real interest rates which floated ever higher compounded debts to unprecedented levels. Simultaneously, sluggish world economic growth hastened the crossover point at which the Third World's debt service costs began to exceed its borrowing capacity. That critical point occurred in the second half of 1982.

Once the crossover point was reached, the structure of sovereign lending became inherently unstable.[7] But it was only when bankers themselves became aware of this instability that the debt crisis exploded in earnest. The decision by the banks to cut back on their exposure to Third World countries threw into further doubt both the ability and the willingness of the borrowers to continue servicing their debts. As a result lending collapsed, particularly to those countries in which bankers sensed trouble. The ratio of interest payments to new loans, which is an indication of the vulnerability to default in the structure of a country's debt, jumped from 0.8 in 1982 to 1.6 in 1983 for the Third World as a whole—and from 0.9 to a dangerous 3.0 for Latin America (see Table 2.1).

Today, the hope of further borrowing can no longer sustain the structure of sovereign lending. Default can be averted only by a combination of sanctions and a new type of "involuntary" lending by bankers.[8] The borrowing country must determine how much capital outflow it is prepared to tolerate in order to avoid sanctions. The banks must determine how much new lending is needed to secure themselves against default. The maximum amount of new money the banks will be prepared to offer to stave off default and the minimum amount which the borrower will require as an inducement to continue interest payments depend in principle on the effectiveness of the potential sanctions against a defaulter, and on the costs of default to the banks.

Thus economists analyzing the theory of sovereign lending today are concentrating on the balancing of costs and sanctions as the central issue in the sovereign debt renegotiations. Game theory suggests that the bargaining advantage is tilted heavily in favor of the debtors.[9] Typical of modern theoretical analysis is the conclusion reached by Paul Krugman that on almost any plausible assumption about sanctions and bargaining methods, "lending to a problem debtor to avoid immediate default is always worthwhile as long as the new lending is less than the debt service."[10] In the real world, though, the three leading Latin-American debtors have received new foreign loans to cover only 30 percent of their interest payments in 1984—and are expected in 1985 to pay an interest bill more than five times larger than their net new borrowing (see Table 2.2).

On the theoretical reasoning, the debtors could clearly be getting a much better deal by threatening default. Yet when the possibility of default has been studied in specific terms, most analysts have concluded that an actual default is unlikely. The most detailed empirical study of default incentives to date, by Thomas Enders and Richard Mattione,[11] found that repudiation of debt was a remotely plausible alternative only for Argentina. For Latin America as a whole, Enders and Mattione concluded that "repudiation is not a better alternative . . . than staying with the reschedulings and stabilization plans"—even though these plans implied, according to their forecasts, that less than one quarter of the continent's interest payments would be covered by new loans between 1983 and 1987; that roughly $150 billion in net capital would be transferred out of the continent in five years; and that the continent's output per capita would still be 7 percent lower by 1987 than it was in 1982 (in Brazil's case per capita output was estimated at roughly 17 percent below its 1982 peak).[12]

Can such a dismal prospect be preferable to default? Is it really so unlikely that major borrowers will decide to deploy the "substantial unexploited bargaining potential"[13] which in theory they clearly possess? Debtors have not yet succeeded in pushing bankers anywhere near the theoretical limits of their involuntary lending capacity for one major reason: they have failed to convince the banks that default is a plausible option, and hence a genuine threat.

If it is assumed that there is no serious prospect of voluntary capital inflows commensurate with projected interest payments being resumed in the foreseeable future,[14] the debtors' wariness of default must mainly reflect a fear of sanctions. But if, on closer examination, legal and political deterrents turn out to be a good deal weaker than generally supposed, a major shift in power could be in store.

Conventional wisdom on the probabilities of default is clearly defined by William Cline in his 1983 study on the debt crisis. After establishing on macroeconomic grounds that "there is an underlying vulnerability in international lending at the present time [because a simple comparison between interest and probable new lending gives] developing countries little incentive to continue honoring debt-servicing obligations,"[15] Cline nonetheless concludes that sanctions make default improbable:

Beyond difficulties with access to . . . credit, defaulting countries could face reprisals. Foreign creditors could attach any of the foreign assets of a defaulting country, as well as its exports abroad (commercial airlines, ships, bank accounts, shipments of commodities and so forth). . . . It is conceivable that if such important countries as Brazil and Mexico declared an indefinite moratorium for reasons of inability to pay, the U.S. government would make no attempt to take reprisals, because of the desire to avoid more permanent jeopardy to political ties. . . . However, private parties would have no access to the type of attachments and interdictions just described, and it would be unlikely that Western governments would actively block the private actors in these efforts.[16]

This conventional wisdom is seriously misleading. None of the reprisals listed by Cline are likely to take effect, at least in the way which he suggests. A defaulter might not get off scot-free—a flagrant repudiation of debt could quite conceivably lead to immensely damaging sanctions, but these would be of a different character and would raise quite different issues from the ones which either debtors or bankers now appear to envisage.

3
The Incentive to Default

Bankers often present the Mexican experience in their show-room, because of the extraordinary $12 billion trade surplus in 1983. Yet the real domestic product of Mexico declined 4 percent in 1983. Adjustment was achieved through import cuts and not by export growth. Only short-sighted analysts can imagine that this is a real success.

—Mario Henrique Simonsen, Minister of Finance of Brazil (1974-79)
World Bank Symposium on International Debt and
Developing Countries, April 1984

Any debtor country considering default must consider two questions: How is its economy likely to perform under the present foreign exchange constraints? And how much foreign exchange can it expect to gain by defaulting? Obviously, default will become a serious policy option only when a debtor country passes the point at which interest on existing loans exceeds the value of expected new lending. But a shortfall in new lending relative to interest payments is not a sufficient condition for default. A country will not default simply to save itself foreign exchange. Desperate measures such as default will not be put on the agenda if a country's prospects look satisfactory without them.

In its 1984 *World Economic Outlook*, the IMF concluded that "developing countries could reasonably [expect] . . . relatively satisfactory rates of growth of imports, exports, and gross domestic product [GDP]" in the rest of the present decade. Specifically, the IMF projected an average growth rate of 4.6 percent a year for the non-oil-developing countries[1] in the six years 1985-90. For the twenty-five biggest borrowers among the LDCs,[2] the projected average growth was somewhat lower: 4.3 percent in 1985-87, rising to 4.4 percent in 1985-90 (see Table 3.1).

These "relatively satisfactory" growth rates, forecast on plausible, if somewhat optimistic, assumptions about international economic conditions (see Table 3.2), have been widely interpreted to mean that the dangers of default should recede rapidly from 1985 onward, as the economies of the debtor countries "bottom out" and their citizens look forward to sustained economic improvement.

Although the 4.3 percent growth rate projected by the IMF for the major borrowers would be well below the 6.5 percent rate these countries reported prior to 1980, it could be sufficient to prevent the buildup of intolerable political pressures. In the absence of such pressures, governments, which are typically averse to taking risks, could be expected to avoid the leap into the unknown which default would constitute.

Obviously if the IMF's external economic assumptions proved over-optimistic, its projections would be less comforting. Nevertheless, a satisfactory base projection, such as the one put forward by the IMF, might leave enough room for maneuver so that any marginal deterioration in the debt problems of some countries could be resolved on the present ad hoc cooperative basis. Unfortunately, the biggest lacuna in the IMF's analysis lies in its assumptions about the availability of bank financing—in effect, the IMF's projections assume away the problems they were designed to illuminate.

The IMF postulates not only that commercial banks will increase their medium-term lending to developing countries by 4 percent from 1986 onward, but also that they will rapidly expand their trade financing; the overall result would be to raise the growth of bank exposures to non-oil LDCs from the rate of 2.6 percent expected in 1985 to 7 percent from 1986 onward.[3] (See Table 3.2.) This reacceleration of bank lending, along with a postulated fall to roughly 9 percent in the interest rates paid by sovereign borrowers, would reduce to a very modest level the developing countries' net transfer of resources to the banks—and this, of course, is the central problem of the debt crisis, as shown in Chapter 2.[4]

If the combination of falling interest rates and voluntary increases in bank lending was realized, it could well succeed in closing the gap between interest rates and new borrowing, thereby genuinely eliminating the danger of default. The trouble is that banks currently appear very unlikely to expand their lending at anything like the rate of 7 percent assumed by the IMF, at least on a voluntary basis. This applies particularly to those countries which are already heavily indebted; most bankers would regard as wildly unrealistic the idea that Brazil will again be borrowing over $7 billion a year in private capital markets from 1986 onward.[5] In fact, extracting this kind of extra financing from unwilling bankers would be precisely the object of a government which threatened to default.

This raises the most serious problem about the IMF's analysis, which emerges from a caveat made by the Fund itself:

It should be borne in mind that the position of certain countries is particularly vulnerable and that a relatively satisfactory outcome for the groups of countries considered in this scenario may mask critical situations in individual cases.[6]

Clearly, the prospects and motivations of political leaders in each of the debtor countries must be analyzed on an individual basis. Since the IMF's longer-term projections for particular countries are never made public, it is necessary to turn to private sector econometric forecasts. In doing so, another point, made only in passing by the IMF, must be emphasized:

Stagnation of output in developing countries *with rapidly growing populations* would be an unacceptable outcome.[7] [emphasis added]

Because of high and differing rates of population growth in many developing countries, economic growth forecasts must always be viewed alongside demographic projections. In political and social terms, it is the per capita growth rate that counts. Moreover, each country's growth rate per capita must be considered in comparison to its growth pattern in the decades before the debt crisis struck. A permanent and major downward departure from such a country's long-term growth path is bound to create political pressures. While there is no evidence that such pressures necessarily provoke political revolutions, they could crystallize much more easily around the less explosive issues of economic nationalism and default. Unlike communism or anti-Americanism, "default" is a slogan that could unite every faction in a Third World country's political spectrum.

When viewed in the light of these considerations, the picture of long-term trends in some of the debtor countries is less reassuring than the one depicted by the IMF's aggregate projections (see Table 3.3).[8] Major disparities between the prospects of individual countries are revealed by the private forecasts, particularly when the per capita growth trends expected for the late 1980s are contrasted with the long-term historic trends (see Table 3.4, column 6). Among the biggest borrowers, one country in particular stands out: Brazil.

Brazil is now in its fourth year of contraction in per capita income. The forecasts suggest that it may still see little per capita growth in 1985, and that even in 1986-89, GDP is unlikely to be growing very much faster than the population.[9] If GDP per capita starts to grow significantly again in the next few years, it will be from a trough some 12 percent below the 1980 level. Had Brazil been able to stay on the pre-crisis growth trend established between 1960 and 1981, GDP per capita would have been nearly 50 percent higher by 1987 than is now forecast. It will take until 1992, according to these forecasts, before per capita output returns to the peak level last seen in 1980. Even more significantly, the country will have to adjust more or less permanently to a growth rate of less than 2 percent per capita. It is questionable whether this can be done given the expectations that were built up during the previous 20-year period of 5.1 percent per capita growth. Whether Brazil's society can maintain its exceptionally unequal income distribution without endangering political stability, in the absence of a rapid rise in general living standards, is the sort of question which will have to be confronted sooner or later.[10]

Which other countries might consider their medium-term outlook to be so gloomy that default could be a tempting alternative?

Asian debtors, with one exception, can look forward to a reasonably prosperous future, with per capita growth rates only slightly below their pre-1981 trends. Neither Korea, Thailand, Malaysia, nor Indonesia are likely to consider default a remotely attractive option, even though Korea's per capita debt is only 20 percent lower than Brazil's. But the Philippines appear to face dismal economic prospects on the basis of current adjustment programs, and desperate remedies cannot be ruled out. Rising political instability fostered by the unpopular regime of President Ferdinand Marcos is only too well illustrated by the chaos that continues to dog him following the murder of opposition leader Benigno Aquino.

Mexico can eventually look forward to a rather stronger recovery than Brazil's, but its recession has been steeper. If the Mexican economy proves to have "bottomed out" in 1983, the recession will have reduced per capita GDP by about 12 percent in just two years. Like Brazilians, Mexicans are unlikely to regain their pre-crisis per capita GDP level until about 1992. They, too, may have to adjust to a per capita growth trend substantially below the historic value of 3.8 percent. (See Table 3.4.) As in Brazil, political pressure seems likely to intensify.

Curiously, Argentina—the third largest Latin-American debtor, and the one that has generated the greatest fears about default—appears to have prospects which are better than most. A long-standing policy of import substitution, which was interrupted only briefly by the mishandled experiment with liberal economics in the late 1970s, has left Argentina with a poor long-term growth performance, but with an economic structure comparatively immune to foreign currency pressures. The Argentine economy, which is self-sufficient in energy and a major food exporter, finds it relatively easy to produce export surpluses and operate without foreign capital inflows. Its medium-term growth prospects seem to be not much worse than they were in the 1960s and 1970s. Argentina's hyperinflation cannot be blamed largely on external pressures, as Brazil's can, since inflation rates of over 200 percent were endemic in Argentina well before the debt crisis. Nevertheless, as the events of early 1984 have shown, a reasonably healthy growth rate does not guarantee a willingness to cooperate fully in servicing debts.

In summary, it seems that economic prospects in Brazil, Mexico, and the Philippines—to name just three of the largest debtors—are not so healthy that the temptation to default can be ruled out. Having been tempted, the second question for the potential defaulter arises: could these prospects be improved by curtailing debt interest payments to foreign banks?

A Cost-Benefit Analysis of Default

Most cost-benefit analyses, whether they refer to the construction of a nuclear power station or the imposition on industry of pollution control laws, attempt to balance quantifiable factors against those which defy precise measurements. Unfortunately, there is no satisfactory way of avoiding certain arbitrary assumptions, particularly in analyzing major events, such as default, where there is no recent experience. Perhaps the best attempt, by Enders and Mattione in their 1984 study, gives projections of economic performance in Latin-American countries based on present policies, and then makes various assumptions about the potential costs of default to provide illustrations of how a total repudiation of debts might affect the economic outlook.

According to their calculations, Argentina, Brazil, Mexico, and Venezuela might all be better off defaulting, provided the total costs imposed by all of the sanctions against a defaulter did not exceed the following levels: the immediate loss of all foreign exchange and gold reserves; a total elimination of all new credit; a permanent addition of 5 percent to the cost of all imports; and a similar permanent reduction in the value of all imports.[11] Even if a 10 percent levy was added to trade costs, Argentina, Brazil, and Venezuela would be better off defaulting—but only if the last two countries could survive with almost no reserves for several years (see Table 3.5).[12]

Because of the confiscation of reserves which they postulated, Enders and Mattione concluded that Argentina would be "the only country fairly sure of surmounting" the 10 percent level of penalties. But for Argentina, the benefits of a default would be quite small: the country's annual growth rate would only increase by 0.6 percentage points. In Brazil, the impact of default on growth trends would be much greater—they would rise by 2 or even 3 percentage points. But Enders and Mattione's calculations showed that Brazil would find it much harder to rebuild adequate foreign exchange reserves and therefore concluded that default by Brazil would be implausible. Prospects for Venezuela and Mexico, the other major debtors whose growth trends might benefit from default, appeared to lie somewhere in between the Brazilian and Argentine cases. In sum, default might not be a rational policy for *every* country in Latin America, but it could well prove attractive to individual debtors, including all of the most important ones, depending on their assessments of the true costs of sanctions.[13]

This suggests not only that a major default could actually occur, but also that the real seriousness of the situation cannot be fully grasped from any kind of clear-cut statistical analysis. The penalties for default are inherently uncertain. Penalties, after all, are likely to be largely political in nature, and attempts to quantify them are almost certain to be misleading. The sanctions against defaulters will either be considerably less costly than the 5 percent of imports and exports postulated by Enders and Mattione, or they will be catastrophically higher. The outcome will depend largely on how the governments of creditor countries respond to default. Potential defaulters are unlikely to try to quantify the costs of defaulting by attaching more or less arbitrary numerical probabilities to the risk of an all-out economic war with the governments of industrial countries. If a political leader feels that he may be ousted if he does not take drastic action, he will not bother much about refined hypothetical calculations about the long-term costs of default—he will try to assess the likelihood of catastrophic retaliation and hold this up against the possible gains from default.

The Maximum Temptation to Default

The first assessment he will make is of the *maximum* foreign exchange gain that his country could hope to secure by defaulting. This can be described as the "maximum temptation to default." Against this temptation, the politician will have to make his judgment about the chances of catastrophic retaliation. This balancing between two incommensurable factors can be performed only through subjective political guesswork. A combination of instinct, experience, opportunism, and passion will determine whether a government is finally overcome by the urge to default. Table 3.6, based on forecasts of the Latin-American economies by Data Resources, Inc. [DRI] and Wharton Econometrics, gives a straightforward reckoning of this temptation.

To illustrate the meaning of the figures, consider the example of Brazil. Between 1985 and 1989, Brazil is expected to pay out an average $13.4 billion a year in interest to all its foreign creditors. Current projections suggest that it can expect to borrow an average of $3.5 billion in new money during the five-year period. This could imply a crude maximum gain of $9.9 billion a year from default. It is realistic to expect, however, that a conciliatory defaulter would continue servicing debts owed to official foreign creditors, such as the IMF, World Bank, and foreign governments. Brazil's official debt service amounts to $0.5 billion a year. In addition, a conciliatory defaulter would probably make a point of maintaining the service of short-term debt in the hope of renewing trade credits. This would require another $0.6 billion annually, leaving $8.8 billion as the maximum foreign exchange gain, a figure that assumes that the defaulter's decision to continue servicing short-term debts dissuades creditors from cutting these off. If short-term debts were lost, Brazil's foreign exchange gain would have to be reduced by a further $4 billion (the estimated level of short-term debt throughout the 1984-87 period), but this would be a once and for all loss, whose repercussions would diminish rapidly after the first year of default. If all this financing was lost in the first year, Brazil's net gain from default would amount to $4.8 billion in the first year, rising to $8.8 billion thereafter.[14]

In the final column of Table 3.6, the maximum foreign exchange saving is compared with the cut in merchandise imports experienced by each country since the peak in economic activity before the debt crisis. This comparison gives a very rough guide to the impact that the maximum gains from default could have on a country's economy. How the additional foreign exchange would affect a country's growth rates depends on the economic policies pursued by the government. The comparisons in the table suggest the freedom to maneuver that default could provide under the most favorable circumstances conceivable: they show the value of additional imports the country could afford to buy each year if it spent nothing on medium-term private debt service. In Brazil's case, 1985 merchandise imports could be increased to more than $24 billion from the $16 billion expected in 1985. This would restore them to more than the peak level of 1980, before Brazil was forced to compress its economy to conserve foreign exchange.

The example of Brazil suggests that the maximum foreign exchange gain from default could be very substantial. It could restore the country's import capacity to its pre-crisis level. But it could not entirely obviate the adjustment policies currently imposed by the IMF. Even if interest on all private foreign debt were entirely eliminated, and if Brazil escaped totally unscathed from any of its creditors' sanctions, it would still be forced to run a substantial and permanent surplus on its merchandise trade account to pay for its deficit on services and for its continuing interest payments to foreign government creditors. Thus, to return imports to the pre-crisis level, Brazil's export drive would have to continue but not, perhaps, with the intensity seen in the past two years.

Table 3.6 shows that very similar considerations apply for several other major borrowers. Under the most favorable possible circumstances, default might allow imports to rise again toward their levels before the debt crises in Argentina, Mexico, and Venezuela. But this would only be possible on condition that exports continued to grow in line with current trends. Alternatively, there could be some relaxation in the export effort, but in that case, there could be no return to 1980 levels of foreign-goods absorption. For Chile, Peru, and the Philippines default appears to offer no way out.

It seems therefore that default *could* be a tempting option for one or more major debtors, depending on what values and probabilities they attach to potential sanctions. Brazil is the country which would probably have least to lose by defaulting, both because its current prospects are poor in relation to past performance and because it is least likely to face serious reprisals from creditor nations, as the following chapters suggest. But other debtors, too, are likely to be tempted.

4
Private Legal Sanctions

A judgment is nothing more than a piece of paper.

—Bruce Nichols, partner, Davis, Polk & Wardwell
University of Illinois Symposium on
Foreign Government Default, 1982

The law is a creditor's most obvious recourse in the event of a default. Various forms of legal redress, such as attachment of assets and seizure of exports, are generally regarded as the ultimate deterrents against default. But bankers' hopes—and borrowers' fears—that crippling costs could be imposed on recalcitrant debtor countries through court action appear to be greatly exaggerated. Western legal systems would give private creditors only modest opportunities to disrupt a defaulting country's trade or to restrain others from doing business with it. There would be little hope of seizing its foreign currency reserves and other assets of its central bank. Even though bankers could hope to create considerable nuisance for a defaulting borrower through private lawsuits, the costs of coping with all this legal trouble would scarcely be commensurable, particularly for a large borrower, with the magnitude of the debt or even the "maximum temptation to default."

The law on sovereign immunity has changed substantially since the days when creditors were completely barred from seeking legal redress against foreign governments. Still, the practical remedies available from lawsuits against sovereign debtors continue to be strictly limited, sometimes by the very statutes which have in principle granted the creditors their rights to bring grievances before the courts. There are a number of reasons why the remedies available to a normal commercial lender are likely to be of limited practical use against sovereign borrowers. In *ascending* order of importance these problems are—immunity, enforcement, incorporation, and tactics.

21

Sovereign Immunity

The traditional doctrine of sovereign immunity, as it was defined in the nineteenth century, was universal and uncompromising in its coverage. As the British lord chancellor asserted in his classic dismissal of a case involving money allegedly misappropriated by the Portuguese government:

> To cite a foreign potentate in a municipal court . . . is contrary to the law of nations and an insult which he is entitled to resent.[1]

This all-encompassing judicial doctrine began to be whittled away over the decades, as sovereign nations became important participants in ordinary commerce and as their commercial behavior became easier to distinguish from their official, governmental acts. The process of attrition, though, was glacial. Even by the 1950s, it was possible to assert that "the doctrine of sovereign immunity presented an absolute bar to suit against any foreign government on defaulted bonds."[2]

It was not until the mid-1970s that the distinction between a nation's commercial activities and its acts as a sovereign power became explicitly enshrined in the laws of the main creditor countries. In 1976, the U.S. Congress approved the Foreign Sovereign Immunities Act (FSIA); in 1978, Britain's Parliament passed the State Immunity Act of 1978 (SIA).[3] In legal theory these acts marked a watershed in relations between sovereign borrowers and lenders. Even so, important vestiges of sovereign immunity have been preserved in American and British law since the passage of these acts, and these are not mere whims of parliamentary draftsmen. They are manifestations of political realities that can be expected to come to the fore again in governmental responses to future defaults.

Diplomacy is a delicate business whose conduct is of great importance to every nation, and the executive branch of government is in general reluctant to allow the random interferences with its international policy which can arise from private litigation against foreign states. A private suit against a foreign government in a U.S. court could, for example, lead to repercussions against U.S. interests within the defendant country. The private plaintiff might be ignorant of and completely indifferent to such external effects, but they could do grave damage to other U.S. citizens, for instance, if the foreign government retaliated against a U.S. judgment by confiscating American assets. Accordingly, governments have always preferred to deny their private citizens legal remedies that could "imperil the amicable relations between governments, and vex the peace of nations," in the words of the U.S. Court of Appeals.[4]

This caveat must be borne in mind in assessing the practical effects of American and British legislation on state immunity. The main significance of the legislation, in the context of sovereign lending, is that it clearly establishes the legal liability of foreign governments for acts which are of a purely commercial nature and gives these governments the right for the first time explicitly to waive their traditional immunities if they wish to do so. Since a refusal to waive immunity in a commercial loan contract can be interpreted by lenders as tantamount to a threat of repudiation, borrowing countries have mostly agreed, with a few notable exceptions[5] to the inclusion of such waivers in loan agreements signed since the passage of these acts.[6]

In principle, therefore, most debtors are now exposed to the judgment of British or American law, and these are the laws which count, since almost all international loan agreements are signed under either United States or English law. The courts of other countries will generally apply whatever nation's law is stipulated in the loan agreement. Thus the doctrine of sovereign immunity in the general form, which made it impossible even "to cite a foreign potentate in a municipal court," is no longer the insuperable obstacle it once was to the legal enforcement of sovereign loan contracts.

There is, however, a further defense which private litigants in the United States may in certain circumstances have to surmount. This is the Act of State principle, an established tenet of U.S. law, which asserts that in certain circumstances American courts will refuse to sit in judgment over the actions of foreign powers, even when these damage private American interests and violate the principles of both U.S. and international law.[7]

This principle has made a dramatic appearance in the most recent court decision on international lending: *Allied Bank v. Banco Credito Agricola de Cartago*.[8] The Supreme Court's classic statement of this principle, in a 1964 case involving an expropriation by the government of Cuba, provides a striking illustration of the profound uneasiness of U.S. courts when confronted with issues touching on foreign policy:

> The doctrine as formulated in past decisions expresses the strong sense of the Judicial Branch that its engagement in the task of passing on the validity of foreign acts of state may hinder rather than further this country's pursuit of goals both for itself and for the community of nations as a whole in the international sphere.[9]

In a more recent case, brought by the U.S. Machinists' Union against OPEC, another federal court spelled out this rationale even more explicitly:

> When the courts engage in piecemeal adjudication of the legality of the sovereign acts of states, they risk disruption of our country's international diplomacy. The Executive Branch may utilize protocol, economic sanctions, compromise, delay and persuasion to achieve international objectives. Ill-timed judicial decisions challenging the acts of foreign states could nullify these tools and embarrass the United States in the eyes of the world.[10]

In the *Allied Bank* case the Court of Appeals' judgment refused to grant relief to Allied, despite an acknowledged default by several Costa Rican banks, on the ground that the default was precipitated by an act of state by the Costa Rican government, in this case in the form of an exchange control decree. A large body of legal opinion holds that this judgment was a serious misinterpretation of the act of state doctrine, and the U.S. Justice Department has recently joined with the plaintiffs in requesting a rehearing.[11] Nevertheless, it is worth noting the following points from the opinions in the *Allied* case for the light which they shed on general attitudes in the federal courts:

> A judgment in favor of Allied in this case would constitute a judicial deter-mination that defendants must make payments contrary to the directives of their government. This puts the judicial branch of the United States at odds with the policies laid down by a foreign government on an issue deemed by that government to be of central importance. Such an act by this court risks embarrassment to the relations between the executive branch of the United States and the government of Costa Rica.[12]

> President Reagan and the Congress reacted sympathetically to Costa Rica's financial crisis and its default on Foreign Assistance Act loans. . . . The House of Representatives also expressed "full support for the Republic of Costa Rica and its democratic institutions as that country responds to the current economic crisis." . . . That Costa Rica's renegotiation of its debts is consistent with our foreign policy is indicated by the support voiced for the renegotiation by both the legislative and executive branches of our govern-ment. . . . Although the actions of Costa Rica affected commercial activi-ty, Costa Rica was clearly acting as a sovereign in preventing a national finan-cial disaster.[13]

If any of these arguments were ultimately upheld by the Supreme Court or echoed by other courts, the legal redress available to international lenders could come to depend explicitly on whether a foreign sovereign enjoyed good relations with the executive and legislative branches of the U.S. government and on where U.S. courts chose to draw the dividing line between "wanton" default and the sort of "warranted" default that takes place in "preventing a national fiscal disaster."

But assuming, as is probable, that an Act of State defense proved ineffective[14] and that effective waivers of sovereign immunity were found to exist in the relevant loan agreements, the creditor would still have to seek enforcement of whatever judgment he might obtain. This is where the banks' real problems would begin. Trying to recoup their money or to impose real hardship on a defaulter would be much easier said than done.

Enforcement Problems

"A judgment is nothing more than a piece of paper," states one of the leading legal authorities on sovereign lending in a recent article on the Foreign Sovereign Immunities Act.[15] A successful suit against a defaulting debtor produces a judgment for the payment of a sum of money. In principle, this judgment can then be enforced by a sheriff or bailiff in a variety of ways. The most effective is normally to seize the debtor's assets, including bank deposits or physical goods (which can then be auctioned). Courts can also order third parties which owe the defaulter money to turn this money over to the bailiffs or plaintiffs. Even without a specific court order, a bank which holds assets (such as deposits) belonging to the defaulter can, on its own initiative, "set off" these deposits against any money which the defaulter may owe it.[16]

But these measures may not work with a sovereign debtor. Recognizing that the forced execution against a foreign sovereign's assets is potentially a more explosive issue than the mere rendering of a "paper" judgment, U.S. and British legislation has in practice guarded immunity from execution more jealously than the general immunity from being cited in a foreign court. Although both the FSIA in the United States and the SIA in Britain allow states to waive their immunity from execution against certain classes of their property, these waivers are subject to important limitations that could often be fatal to the aggrieved creditors' hopes of winning substantial recovery or causing serious commercial harm to the defaulting sovereign.[17]

First, even where the state has signed a specific waiver, the FSIA allows execution only against property which is "used for commercial activity in the United States."[18] This means that assets clearly used for governmental purposes, including diplomatic and military property, cannot be attached under any circumstances. It also leaves open the question of commercial property not used in the United States. Second, property held by a central bank "for its own account" is not covered by a general waiver. The foreign government or its central bank must "explicitly" waive the special immunity enjoyed by central banks.[19]

In addition, there is in general nothing to stop a defaulter from moving his property outside U.S. jurisdiction in anticipation of an adverse judgment, unless his creditors can persuade the courts to grant a "prejudgment attachment" at the time they first bring their suit. Since a prejudgment attachment is potentially an even more provocative act in diplomatic terms than a seizure of sovereign property after a judgment is rendered, the FSIA narrows even further the conditions in which attachments are allowed. Again it requires an "explicit" waiver of prejudgment attachment to be written into the loan agreement.[20] More important, the FSIA does not recognize any such waiver for the property of a foreign central bank. Thus, it is improbable that central bank property, including foreign exchange and gold reserves, could be attached prior to judgment.

In most cases, the central bank's assets are likely to be by far the most important foreign assets belonging specifically to the *government* of a sovereign country. Although, by definition, such assets are no more than a minor part of creditors' claims, the loss of reserves could cause serious disruption for a debtor country. In the detailed analysis of the costs and benefits of default by Enders and Mattione,[21] the postulated loss of all foreign exchange reserves was the most important explanation of the negative results of debt repudiation. If governments could protect their reserves from confiscation, then the Enders and Mattione approach suggests that default would be an unambiguously attractive option for Argentina, Brazil, Venezuela, and probably Mexico (see Table 3.5). Hence, the special immunity enjoyed by central bank assets could be critical to an evaluation of the default option.

The FSIA stipulates that central banks are absolutely protected from prejudgment attachments, irrespective of waivers that may have been given by central bankers or their governments.[22] In practice, the special immunity would be of no avail for reserves held in private commercial banks, since these banks could simply "set off" such reserves against any loan in default. As most foreign central banks keep their funds with the Federal Reserve Bank of New York, they should be secure and serviceable for the defaulting country, at least until a U.S. court delivers final judgment against the default. In fact, the State Department and the New York Fed have repeatedly made representations to the courts urging that "the immunities provided in the FSIA should be broadly construed."[23] It seems, therefore, that creditors would face a steep uphill struggle in attaching or immobilizing the foreign exchange and gold reserves held in the United States by a defaulting country.[24]

Even if such an attachment looked like a serious threat, the foreign central bank would have a number of more secure options. Deposits at

The Bank for International Settlements in Basle are absolutely "immune from seizure or attachment" under article 55 of the BIS statutes, which are recognized by both Swiss and international law.[25] Holdings of Special Drawing Rights at the IMF are also protected under all circumstances. And, while the State Immunity Act in Britain does not offer foreign central banks unconditional protection in cases where immunity has been specifically waived by the bank or its government, Mareva injunctions (the English law equivalent of prejudgment attachments) have never been imposed in cases involving foreign states and central banks.[26] In addition, there is no shortage of Swiss, Caribbean, and other offshore banks which have no significant involvement in the sovereign lending business and would be happy to operate anonymous or nominee accounts, effectively outside any legal jurisdiction, on behalf of foreign central banks.

Suppose, nevertheless, that a judgment *could* be executed against the assets of a foreign sovereign—and even against a portion of the central bank's foreign currency reserves. How much harm would this do to a defaulting nation, assuming realistically that the foreign assets actually owned by the state are miniscule in comparison with the servicing costs of the foreign debt? At this point an even bigger obstacle arises to effective legal relief.

The Veil of Incorporation

Many participants in international banking appear to believe that creditors could bring a defaulting country's trade almost to a standstill by attaching defaulter's ships, airplanes, and export cargoes whenever they ventured into the jurisdiction of a nation prepared to recognize the judgment of a U.S. or English court (depending on which law governs the loan agreement in default). Such a belief, exemplified in the comments by Cline quoted above and sometimes fostered by U.S. and European government officials, is unrealistic. Individual citizens of a country—including corporate citizens—are in no way liable for the debts of their government. The courts will never punish a private Argentine wheat exporter or a private Brazilian airline, for example, for the defaults of their states.

In truth, the principle that a judgment against a particular entity can be enforced only against that entity's own assets goes much further than a mere distinction between private individuals and their governments.[27] Nationalized corporations, wholly owned by the government and central banks, are recognized by the courts of most countries as distinct legal entities, separate from their government and liable only for their own defaults. Even in judgments involving Communist countries, where the functional identity between the state and its economic organs might appear to be the very essence of the political system, courts have usually decided that state trading monopolies had to be carefully distinguished from the governments that owned them:

> State-controlled enterprises, with legal personality, ability to trade and enter contracts of private law, though wholly subject to the control of the state, are a well-known feature of the modern commercial scene. The distinction between them, and their governing state, may appear artificial: but it is an accepted distinction in the law of England and other states.[28]

This doctrine, sometimes known as "the veil of incorporation," is subject to only one type of general exception in U.S. courts: "Under general principles of American law, the corporate form of an entity will not be disregarded unless the corporate form has been used to perpetrate a fraud or the corporation's owners have so dominated or disregarded the corporate form that the corporation primarily transacted the owner's business rather than its own corporate business."[29]

There have been a small number of cases where the defaults of one government body have led to attachments of assets used by another arm of the government; these have mostly involved property which turned out to have been owned by the state itself. In the most famous such case, Morgan Guaranty's attachment through the German courts of Iran's stake in Fr. Krupp AG, the shares were owned by the government of Iran.[30] Thus it would almost certainly be futile for a government's aggrieved creditors to pursue the assets of private traders or even of state-owned entities from the country in question unless those entities are actually cosignatories or guarantors of the loan contracts in default.

Admittedly, there could be a significant field of action against those countries where part of the debt is in fact contracted by nationalized industries, such as state oil and trading companies. Creditors of nationalized companies might well attempt to seize any of their assets which might come into the jurisdiction of a sympathetic court. In some cases, such assets might be quite substantial. Creditors could also attempt to attach or garnish debts owed *to* defaulting nationalized trading companies by importers in the United States, Britain, and other creditor countries. But a nation planning to default could also take care to organize its international trading arrangements and its domestic corporate structures so that assets belonging to vulnerable public sector corporations were not exposed abroad. It could continue servicing those debts in which its international trading corporations were specifically involved. It could sell certain exports for cash only, so that receivables in creditor countries were not exposed to attachment. And it could ensure that the legal title to its exports passed to foreign customers as soon as the goods were loaded for shipment. The last precaution would not be difficult to take since, in any case, it is already standard practice in important areas of international trade. Mexico's oil exports, for example, become the legal property of a foreign oil purchaser the moment they pass the flange of the customer's tanker. Similar arrangements make invulnerable Argentina's wheat exports.

The visions which some bankers appear to have of freezing a defaulter's entire foreign trade by means of legal attachments seem to be like embers in the air. Litigation would be vexatious and would impose costs on the defaulter. For many borrowers, the uncertain penalties for default would have to be enormous before they outweighed the large and obvious financial benefits of lifting the burden of debt. Thus it would seem that the legal sanctions available to private creditors could hardly be a decisive consideration in a sovereign borrower's decision whether or not to default.

What is more, the legal cards are stacked even more heavily against the creditors than is suggested by a mere assessment of the judicial penalties for default. For banks might decide not to turn to the courts.

Tactical Considerations

In deciding what action to take in the event of a default, banks would have to weigh not just the limited penalties they could hope to impose on the borrower and the small financial compensation they could hope to extract from attachments and asset sales. They would also have to consider the costs of their litigation. This does not refer to lawyers' fees, court costs, and possible damages for wrongful attachments. Substantial though all these might be, they would be negligible in relation to the indirect costs—which some banks might bear if they chose to seek judicial sanctions. Indeed, far from benefiting from legal action, some banks could actually lose more than the defaulter—even if their legal actions were to succeed.

Legal actions against a defaulter, particularly if they resulted in the seizure of significant assets, could turn a conciliatory default into an outright repudiation. The indignation provoked by seizures of assets could result in the defaulting government declaring its unwillingness to honor its debts as a matter of principle, even if it could find the resources to do so. Such a repudiation might require the banks to write off as a total loss the whole of a nation's debt. In a conciliatory default, when the debtor nation continues to recognize its ultimate responsibility for some debt repayment, the amount that has to be written off is open to much wider interpretation by bankers, auditors, and regulatory agencies. In addition, an escalation of hostilities between debtors and creditors would undermine the ability of the borrowing countries to continue with what limited debt service it was prepared to undertake in a conciliatory default. Finally, repudiation would almost certainly provoke retaliatory action by the defaulting country against the business interests of the creditor banks within its own borders. For some of the major banks, this could be a very substantial threat.

The potentially daunting indirect costs of legal action to the banks should be weighed against some major indirect benefits. For the biggest banks, the preservation of order in the international banking business depends to some extent on a perceived willingness to use legal sanctions as a last resort. For some small banks, on the other hand, litigation could provide an instrument of blackmail with which to extract special treatment from the larger banks, which would fear the consequences of an uncontrolled legal escalation.[31]

Taking all these direct and indirect costs and benefits together, legal action would not appear to be a very serious menace for a major borrower considering default; debtors as big as Brazil, Mexico, Argentina, or Venezuela might rationally consider such a threat to be like a bluff in a poker game.

Against these theoretical arguments there are, however, two recent episodes of legal sanctions, attachments, and asset seizures which bankers and lawyers have sometimes presented as cautionary tales to the recalcitrant debtors of today. These are the bank and external asset freezes imposed on Iran in 1980 and Argentina in 1982.[32] It is sometimes asked how these sanctions could have been successfully imposed if sovereign nations, central banks, and foreign entities of various kinds really enjoyed the ample legal protection described above. The explanation of this apparent paradox is simple and telling.

The sanctions against Iran in the United States and the British freeze on Argentine assets were both primarily political acts performed directly by the American and British governments. Although the U.S. courts allowed some attachments of Iranian government property by private litigants during the hostage crisis of 1980, the major sanction was the freeze on all Iranian assets on November 14, 1979. This was not ordered by any court and had nothing to do with any private citizen's legal grievance. It was a quintessentially governmental action, taken by President Jimmy Carter under the International Emergency Economic Powers Act. Similarly, the blocking of Argentine bank accounts in Britain was a political decision taken by the Cabinet in response to an act of war and implemented not through the judicial system but by order under the Exchange Control Act.

A comparison between the tortuous processes of civil litigation required by the Foreign Sovereign Immunities Act or the State Immunity Act and the peremptory effectiveness of the Iranian or Argentine asset freezes illustrates perfectly a central theme of this analysis: the political branches of creditor country governments have almost limitless powers to deploy against defaulting debtors, if they so desire. Such governmental reprisals cannot even be circumscribed by current laws or precedents, since it is always in the power of Parliament or Congress to change the laws (including those governing sovereign immunity) if they see fit.

It would be possible for European or American *governments* to seize a defaulter's assets, to impose a trade embargo, to force its expulsion from the World Bank and other international aid agencies, to break off diplomatic relations, or even to declare war. But would the creditor governments choose to do so? Why should they? Would they regard a "justified default" by Brazil or even a "wanton default" by Argentina in the same light as the Ayatollah Khomeini's kidnapping of diplomats or General Galtieri's Falklands invasion?

To pose these questions is to see why the debt crisis cannot be viewed simply as a dispute between private bankers and foreign debtors. If a default occurs, the debt issue will move rapidly into the diplomatic and political arena. The responsibility will then rest with politicians. They could precipitate an international economic disaster, or they could find an amicable solution which served the interest of debtor and creditor countries alike.

5
Private Nonjudicial Sanctions

You know you have several years of bad business, but then you have to consider, if you pull through, how hard it will be to reestablish yourself in the market. We're back to long-term versus short-term decision making.

—Nicholas Tournillon, Treasurer of GTE International Inc.,
on operating in Latin America[1]

If the threat of litigation is hardly a wild card in the poker game between private creditors and potential defaulters, creditors do have another, potentially stronger card. This is the disruption of financial and trading flows through nonjudicial commercial sanctions.

One of the misconceptions which arises from failing to distinguish between conciliatory default and provocative repudiation is the belief that all the foreign economic interests in a debtor country will unite in boycotting it if it defaults. In reality, they may have no incentive to do so; for a default on medium-term bank debts which was carefully planned and presented in a conciliatory manner could leave unscathed the interests of foreign traders, multinational direct investors, and providers of trade finance. In ideal circumstances, a default could even benefit foreign equity investors and traders if it succeeded in lifting the foreign currency constraint on the economy's growth.

Even in such a conciliatory default, multinational companies and traders from the creditor countries might try to inflict damage on the defaulting country, either out of a sense of solidarity with the banks or out of a desire to promote the rule of law in international financial transactions. However, past experience—in defaults, nationalizations, and even revolutions—does not suggest that such action is particularly likely. Managers of multinational companies point out that bankers have rarely refused to do business with countries which had expropriated industrial, oil, or mining companies—for example, in Libya, the Middle East, Peru, and even Cuba.[2]

The attitudes of multinationals to their host countries are determined mainly by the way their own industries are treated. A default on bank debts would be regarded as alarming mainly if it augured a broader movement toward economic xenophobia. That might take place, of course, but it is by no means a certainty. Thus, in analyzing the nonjudicial sanctions which a defaulter might suffer from the private sector of creditor countries, it is important to identify those interests who have the potential for imposing sanctions and to weigh their motivations and the prospects that they would take action.[3]

There are four major groups, with considerable overlap between them, which could conceivably impose sanctions: medium-term lenders, direct equity investors, traders in ordinary (nonfinancial) goods and services, and providers of trade finance.

Medium-Term Lenders

For medium-term lenders, the issue is fairly clear-cut. A default on bank debts would almost certainly cut a country off from new medium-term bank financing for a substantial period, perhaps a decade or more. Still, the probable loss of medium-term bank financing is not in itself a major threat for a country which has decided to take a look over the precipice of default. If there was hope of obtaining such financing in the foreseeable future on a level comparable to the cost of debt servicing, the country would not be considering default in the first place.

Even on optimistic assumptions, some of the major debtors have no reasonable expectations, at least for the next few years and probably for the next decade, of obtaining capital inflows *larger than their total debt service payments.*[4] In the much longer term, extending, say, twenty-five or thirty years ahead, there is no evidence that a country's past defaults significantly affect the level of new financing available. In this connection, it is worth remembering that nearly every one of today's major problem debtors had already defaulted massively on sovereign debts in the 1930s. Cuba, one of the few countries which actually repudiated its debts in this century, was receiving small amounts of medium-term financing from European governments and banks within ten years of its default on obligations to American creditors.[5]

Equity Investors

The only generalization which can be made about equity investors is that their decisions will be motivated mainly by the country's prospects for long-term economic growth and by the degree of security offered to foreign investors. While this latter criterion could easily be jeopardized by a government which turned a default on bank debts into a general attack against foreign economic interests, there is no necessary reason why this should happen, especially if a conciliatory default met with a conciliatory response from the United States and other creditor governments.

At present, multinationals operating in countries such as Mexico, Brazil, Nigeria, and even Argentina do not appear to think that they would be threatened with expropriation in the event of a default on bank debts. They could, of course, find themselves threatened if an aggressive response by creditors found support in the creditor countries' courts and governments, and led to serious judicial or political reprisals. The threat that, "If you take one bag of our coffee, we will take Ford, Volkswagen, and General Motors,"[6] expressed by one political commentator in Brazil, would probably be endorsed by the politicians and armed forces of many debtor nations. But the very potential for international political conflagration could lead American and European courts to tread carefully over a debtor nation's sensitivities—and to deny creditors the kinds of remedies which might provoke debtor countries into expropriating foreign equity investments. Brazil, for example, is the largest market outside Europe and North America for many multinationals. For some, including Volkswagen and Fiat, Brazil ranks second only to the home market.

In recent years, the multinationals *have* drastically curtailed their investment activities in the debtor countries. But this curtailment has had less to do with fears of expropriation than with the grim economic environment in most of the countries in question. In particular, multinationals cite[7] the collapse of demand in domestic markets, the rationing of foreign exchange for imports, and the restrictions placed on dividend repatriation. All of these handicaps are largely attributable to foreign exchange shortages. If a default could succeed in lifting these shortages, without unleashing an attack on foreign economic interests generally, it might even be welcomed, at least in private, by some industrial investors. If such a default succeeded in improving a country's long-term growth prospects, it could even increase the inflow of foreign direct investment over the long run. The backlog of multinational investment projects which have been cancelled during the past few years in countries such as Brazil and Nigeria as a result of the economic crises, could produce a bigger boom in new investment than is generally expected if economic conditions clearly started improving.[8]

One special group of equity investor needs to be considered separately: the major international banks, which have invested billions of dollars in establishing major local banking operations within some of the debtor countries. The banks with large local business interests—the outstanding example is Citicorp in Brazil—have relationships with these countries in which the long-term interest of permanent equity investors sometimes vies with the medium-term lenders' simpler and more detached concern about timely debt repayment. For some of the multinational banks, the local operations are so large and profitable—Citicorp, for example, earned 22 percent of its worldwide net income in Brazil during 1981-83 and its net return on assets there was nearly five times the U.S. level[2]—that if a conciliatory default took place, the bank might regard the preservation and expansion of its local operations as deserving a higher priority than any quest for judicial or economic reprisals.

Trade and Trade Credit

The largest and most important category of private agents whose actions could have an impact on the debtor countries is the companies which trade in goods and services, and which also may be major direct investors. Apart from legal obstacles which the banks may succeed in throwing up against trade with a defaulter, there seem to be only two plausible reasons why importers or exporters in America, Europe, Japan, or elsewhere would refrain from doing business as usual with a country defaulting on its medium-term debts.

The first would be open or covert governmental action taken in retaliation for the default—an official trade embargo, the erection of protectionist barriers against the defaulting country's exports, or perhaps informal government guidance in favor of an unofficial trade boycott. Such sanctions could potentially be disastrous for a defaulter, and they are at the heart of the fears of debtor countries about default.

They are, however, essentially political acts outside the control of private creditors or other economic agents. (These sanctions will be analyzed in detail in chapters 6 and 7.) The second method of impeding trade is in the hands of the private sector and is a weapon which the banks may well be in a position to wield. The interruption of trade finance might turn out to be the heaviest penalty for a defaulter.

Trade finance is a critical issue because most trade is conducted on a credit basis of one kind or another. A common rule of thumb is that a country's lines of trade credit may cover as much as six months' merchandise imports and should at a minimum cover about three months. A debtor country which lost the whole of this trade finance would find it a daunting sum to recoup. For a few potential defaulters this loss could almost outweigh the immediate gains from nonpayment of interest on medium-term debts (see Table 5 1), so that trade finance could be the Achilles' heel of a default strategy. There are, however, some mitigating factors.

The loss of trade credits is a once-and-for-all cost, which cannot really be compared with the recurring benefit of lifting the medium-term interest burden. Debtor countries have already been forced by the lack of trade finance to move much of their trade onto a cash basis. Moreover, a significant amount of trade finance could probably be retained even after a default on medium-term debts. Much of this finance is provided not by foreign banks but by foreign suppliers or specialized trade-credit institutions. Like direct investors, their business policies will generally be guided by their own experience as well as by the treatment accorded the medium-term bank creditors.[10]

A country which defaulted on its medium-term debt might therefore try to split its trade creditors from its medium-term lenders by providing its importers with the foreign exchange needed to service their trade credits as they fell due. The hope would be that trade credits whose full service was maintained would be renewed. This, in effect, has been the strategy which nearly all the debtor countries, with the exception of Nigeria, have followed.[11] While they have delayed and rescheduled payments on medium-term bank debts, they have continued to service trade debts fairly promptly. As a result of this reasonably favorable experience, government export-credit agencies are still insuring short-term supplier credits to all but a handful of the debtor countries, and some private suppliers are willing to continue exporting on credit terms.

If the defaulting government could persuade suppliers that more, rather than less, foreign exchange would be available after a default for the servicing of trade, it could have a reasonable chance of retaining some of its credit lines. Multinational companies trading with their own subsidiaries in the defaulting country would be particularly likely to maintain credit lines, assuming they did not decide to pull out of the country altogether.[12] Some government export credit institutions, whose credit policies are governed by their own loss experience, might also continue to offer short-term cover to their national exporters, if the default was of a nonprovocative type which could be tacitly accepted by the creditor government in question.[13]

Trade credits provided directly by foreign banks almost certainly would be cut off. But if the defaulting country did not block repayment of such debts, and instead maintained full service of all its trade debts in a nondiscriminatory manner, the debtor country could foster an image of "good faith" in international financial and diplomatic circles. That, in turn, might accelerate the breakdown of solidarity among the banks in opposition to its default.[14] Practically speaking, it might not take very long for a country which defaulted on medium-term debt but maintained prompt service on its trade debts to rehabilitate itself in the trade financing market. The solidarity among bankers could rapidly begin to crumble for several reasons.

Most important, short-term trade financing is a highly profitable and not very risky business if it is conducted on a genuinely self-liquidating basis. Some banks will eventually come forward to claim these profits, if they can be convinced of a country's ability and willingness to pay trade creditors in preference to medium-term lenders. Banks with little or no exposure to the country's defaulted medium-term debts will be all the more willing to step into the breach left by those which are overexposed.[15]

Furthermore, several of the biggest bank lenders to the potential defaulters have very substantial and profitable long-term equity interests in these countries' domestic banking markets. If they wish to continue local operations, these banks will come under very strong pressure to assist their customers with trade financing.

Finally, trade financing is as much a service provided to the exporter who wants to sell goods to, say, Brazil, as it is to the Brazilian importer. By refusing trade financing to Brazil, banks would be hurting their clients, the exporters of America, Europe, and Japan. Not only would these exporters mount pressure on their governments to revive officially guaranteed trade finance, they would also seek out private bankers who were willing to finance trade with the defaulter as soon as it became clear that the country's liquidity situation had improved sufficiently to make trade financing self-liquidating. In the fierce competition among bankers for corporate customers, this consideration could be quite powerful.

Consequently, in the absence of political sanctions by creditor governments, the permanent damage to trade could be controlled and minimized by a conciliatory defaulter. If the government managed to maintain prompt payments on any trade credits which were not cut off, other credit lines could gradually reopen. Thus, it is unlikely that the private sector alone could or would impose a large and permanent additional cost on a defaulting country's trade, as assumed by Enders and Mattione, for example. It would be another matter if creditor country governments decided to launch a deliberate attack on the country's economy in retaliation for default.

6
The Economic Consequences of Default

It is no secret that over the years a lot of intellectual capital has been invested in the proposition that massive defaults in the Third World will cause a world financial crisis. Those who have taken that view since 1973-74 have been proved wrong, and those of us who believed the market would work proved correct.

—Walter Wriston, former chairman of Citicorp,
American Bankers Association,
International Monetary Conference, 1981

Creditor governments have sometimes responded to default with full-scale military invasions; occasionally, they have imposed receivership on central banks and customs sheds in debtor countries; and at other times, they have done nothing. In one memorable episode, an American president even offered a public apology to a defaulting country for the greed and "super-salesmanship" of U.S. banks.[1]

In general, the forcefulness of the response has diminished steadily with the waning of the imperialist era. But the main lesson suggested by historical experience is that the diplomatic protection and political assistance that a creditor can expect from his government depends less on the extent of the injustice he has suffered than on the government's assessment of its own foreign policy priorities and strategic needs.[2]

In practice during the past half-century, this has usually meant that creditor governments have taken no action—except in a few cases where physical assets have been flagrantly expropriated by states whose ideology was anyway repugnant to the interests of the creditor governments involved.[3] Nevertheless, the potential threats posed by creditor government retaliation are enormous, and these threats are undoubtedly the most powerful deterrent to default.

The arsenal of potential sanctions available to the United States, Britain, and other creditor countries is almost unlimited. To be sure, the use of armed might against a defaulter is unthinkable today, but because of the world's increasing interdependence, economic and political sanctions of other kinds—for example, trade embargoes; exclusion from international institutions, such as the IMF or World Bank; or the loss of development aid or military assistance—could be as effective as the nineteenth century's gunboats in bringing defaulters to their knees.[4]

A total embargo on trade, covering the defaulter's imports as well as exports, would be disastrous. It would cripple the import-export industries of countries such as Mexico and Brazil and throw their economies into depressions even deeper than the slumps they are currently suffering. A one-way trade ban, which blocked only the defaulter's exports, would alone have a serious effect. The country's capacity to import would be reduced to the extent that its loss of exports exceeded its foreign exchange gains from default.[5]

But *would* the United States and other creditor governments impose trade bans and other sanctions against a defaulter? Why would they wish to do so? And how would such actions affect the creditor nations' own economies and political objectives? These are the questions on which the future of the debt problem could hinge.

The considerations that creditor country governments will weigh in their responses to a foreign default can be broken down into three broad categories: effects on their own economies; effects on various domestic political constituencies; and effects on economic, political, and ideological interests in the defaulting country and the world at large.

Impact on the United States Economy

The first and foremost concern of the U.S. government* if a default actually occurred would be to prevent the collapse of the American economy. If the economy plunged into depression as a result of a defaulter's action, the public outcry would probably dictate retaliatory action whether it was in the national interest or not.

Recent simulations by Data Resources Inc. (DRI) and Wharton Econometrics have suggested that a default by the whole of Latin America would cost the United States nearly 2.5 percent of gross national product (GNP) in lost output and 1.1 million jobs within one year. A default by Brazil alone, according to DRI, would cost 0.8 percent and 399,000 jobs, while a default by Argentina would be far less damaging—0.2 percent of GNP in output and 90,000 jobs (see Table 6.1).[6]

_____

*For the sake of simplicity, I focus on the likely actions of the U.S. government; other creditor nations can be expected to respond on broadly similar lines.

The nasty consequences of default stem, in their analyses, from two separate causes in roughly equal measure—further weakening of the banking system and the impact on U.S. exports of a collapse in the defaulter's ability to buy foreign goods.

The adverse effects of a default on U.S. exports are easy enough to understand, but only if it is assumed that trade credits are cut off or sanctions imposed. As explained earlier,* there is no reason why U.S. exports to a defaulting country should suffer in the absence of such developments. Some reductions in trade financing would be inevitable after a default, but they might well be offset by the defaulter's enlarged capacity to make cash purchases: to increase imports is, after all, the main point of defaulting from the defaulter's point of view. Thus the loss of U.S. exports, which might represent about half the economic damage of default, could be readily avoided if the U.S. government avoided aggressive policies toward a conciliatory defaulter.[7]

The banking impact of default would be more complex and less readily managed. The top U.S. banks have loans out to the six major problem debtors equal to nearly 180 percent of their capital (see Table 6.3). If all, or even one, of these countries defaulted, the immediate threat would be a run on the banks, leading to illiquidity and ultimately even insolvency, as the banks scrambled for cash to repay depositors. Even if banks succeeded in preserving confidence among their depositors, there could be, in the slightly longer term, an abrupt contraction of credit, leading to economic recession. A credit contraction would take place if a major part of the banking system's capital were wiped out, forcing banks to call in bank loans in order to preserve statutory reserve ratios. The effect could, in principle, be devastating, since the one-to-twenty ratio of capital to assets required for large U.S. banks implies a credit contraction twenty times as great as the loss of banking equity.[8] The most important question, therefore, in assessing the impact of a default on the U.S. economy, and in predicting how the government might respond to it, is how the banks would fare in the event of default.

Could the Banks Survive Default?

In principle, the Federal Reserve System can maintain the liquidity of any or all banks hit by a default. The Fed can lend, lend boldly, and go on lending, in the words of Walter Bagehot (cited recently by Preston Martin, the vice-chairman of the Fed, during the Continental Illinois

---

*See Chapter 5.

crisis),[9] to a bank afflicted by a temporary loss of confidence. The backing of the banking system was made surprisingly explicit in September 1984, when the comptroller of the currency acknowledged that regulators would not allow the top eleven U.S. banks to fail.[10] Although the Fed cannot legally lend to a bank that is insolvent, the U.S. government could preserve even insolvent banks by providing them with temporary injections of capital, as it did in the recent case of Continental Illinois.

Theoretically, the authorities could even maintain the liquidity of the banking system without running the risk either of multiple credit contractions or of inflationary expansion of the money supply. By balancing open market sales of Treasury bills judiciously against emergency lending and capital injections to the distressed banks, the money supply could be prevented from rising or falling outside its target zone. In the Continental Illinois rescue, the Fed achieved precisely this result, counterbalancing its emergency lending to Continental almost dollar for dollar with reductions in the availability of nonborrowed reserves (see Table 6.2). In a more general crisis, though, there might well be a case for a temporary upward adjustment of monetary growth targets in the event of default, to compensate for the increase in the public's precautionary demand for money.[11]

But even in a world of perfectly skilled Federal Reserve and Treasury officials, the problem of bank solvency, as opposed to liquidity, would raise broader issues. Capital injections from the federal government are not a satisfactory way of permanently preserving the solvency of the banks, since in the United States at least, the nationalization of a major part of the banking system is considered politically undesirable. Thus, after the immediate liquidity crisis was over, new private capital would need to be brought into the banking system to replace the stake of the federal government. This is precisely the problem which confronted the Federal Deposit Insurance Corporation (FDIC) in the Continental Illinois rescue and which has led to the quasi-nationalization of what used to be the country's eighth largest bank.

Nevertheless, a recapitalization of the banking system by private sector investors might be possible after a default. Two major misconceptions about the debt crisis frequently arise on this point. Large banks currently find it difficult and costly to raise capital in the equity market, and the FDIC had to abandon its search for a buyer for Continental Illinois; but this does not imply a permanent shortage of equity capital available for investment in the U.S. banking industry.

Banking stocks, and especially the shares of the larger international banks, have been out of favor in the stock market in recent years because investors have considered reported earnings and solvency positions of the big banks to be extremely precarious, largely as a result of their foreign exposure. But there is no lack of capital readily available for investment in U.S. *domestic* banking, as evidenced by the rush to take advantage of bank deregulation by interstate bank holding companies, savings and loans, insurance companies, and nonfinancial corporations.[12] A forced contraction of credit by the major banks exposed to sovereign lending would, in principle, only add to the profitable opportunities in the domestic banking market.

A second misconception is that the whole of the U.S. banking system is threatened by the debt crisis. The exposure of banks to foreign loans falls off rapidly with size; below the top ten banks there are few banks whose foreign exposures exceed their total primary capital (see Table 6.4). There are nearly 15,000 commercial banks in the United States, and the top ten constitute less than 20 percent of this market by assets and an even smaller proportion in terms of capital.[13] Even the total elimination of all the money center banks could, in theory, leave most of the U.S. banking industry's capital unharmed, provided deposits in the interbank market were protected by the federal government. In congressional hearings, the House Banking Committee reported that if Continental Illinois had been allowed to fail, only twenty some banks would have been brought down with it—hardly the nationwide collapse once feared.[14]

In theory, therefore, it would appear that the capital base of the U.S. domestic banking industry could be rebuilt rapidly by new investors or by the expansion of existing financial institutions which were not involved in foreign lending, even if the *present* shareholders in the big international banks were to lose all their money in sovereign loan write-offs.

In practice, of course, the transition from a partially insolvent banking system overexposed to sovereign loans to a well-capitalized domestic system would not be accomplished so smoothly. In the unlikely event of a complete repudiation of all sovereign debts, the loss of bank capital might be so great, particularly if the situation was badly handled by the monetary authorities, that a long interval of federal government control over several major banks would be inevitable. Furthermore, losses beyond the present magnitude of the banks' capital would still have to be borne by someone—either bank depositors or the government. If the government refused to bear these losses and uninsured depositors forfeited their funds, insolvencies could spread through the interbank market to smaller banks which were not directly involved in sovereign lending. As a result, a genuine financial panic could engulf the whole American economy.

Such a catastrophe is quite unlikely. Given a reasonable level of competence and pragmatic action by the authorities, there would be no reason for domestic banking to come to a halt even if the present shareholders in a small number of major banks were wiped out altogether as a result of their foreign exposure.

In reality, the U.S. government and monetary authorities would presumably do their utmost to avoid such dramas. With prompt and flexible policies they could probably succeed in rescuing even the most exposed money center banks, particularly in the event of a *conciliatory* default.

The commonly quoted ratios of bank exposure to capital exaggerate the vulnerability of the banking system. As already noted, the small banks are much less exposed than the money centers. More important, a conciliatory default would allow the money center banks to avoid writing off more than a small part of their exposures to defaulting countries, and to spread these losses over an extended period.

Confidence, Conciliation, and Cash Flow

In a purely abstract world, it might be possible for banks with 100 percent of their capital exposed to Third World countries to continue doing business as usual even if all sovereign borrowers totally repudiated their loans. This conjuring trick could be performed, provided there was no loss of confidence by depositors, for the very reason which led to the debt crisis in the first place: the banks are no worse off, in terms of cash flow, if a debtor stops paying interest altogether, than if the debtor pays his interest with one hand, only to borrow it back with the other. This is precisely what happened in the five years between 1978 and 1983. The banks received about $125 billion in interest from developing countries and then advanced the very same countries $140 billion in "new money."

So long as the banks could expand their deposits more rapidly than the rate of interest they paid to existing depositors, this kind of arrangement could continue. The constraint on their ability to do so is the possibility that depositors, realizing that their money is unsupported by sound assets, panic and withdraw their funds. In the 1970s, there was no danger of this occurring because loans to developing countries were generally considered safe. Whether a default would precipitate panic withdrawals would depend in the short term on the amount of support offered by the Federal Reserve System. In the slightly longer term, however, confidence even in the Fed's assurances would collapse if it appeared that banks were being permitted to go on trading after their capital bases had been effectively wiped out.

Whether depositors and investors could be convinced to keep their money with the banks in question might depend largely on how default was presented, by both the debtors and the U.S. government.

An outright repudiation by the debtors might make it impossible for monetary authorities to persuade depositors that the major banks remained truly solvent. The borrowers' refusal to accept liability for interest or capital repayments would strongly imply that a large proportion of the assets in the banks' balance sheets were almost worthless. Even in such extreme circumstances, bank managements and examiners would probably argue that a future government might renew some debt servicing, but depositors would presumably treat such claims with skepticism.[15]

By contrast, conciliatory default might appear far less disastrous. If the government of a defaulting country publicly expressed its intention to renew debt servicing at some time in the foreseeable future,[16] a strong argument could be made by bank managements, auditors, and regulators that the assets in question should be kept in the balance sheet at something approaching their full value, pending clarification of the borrower's willingness and ability to pay. The value of the defaulted loans could then be written down gradually, over a period of years or even decades, to the amount which lenders could ultimately hope to realize. In practice, the banks would do this by cutting into their reported profits to increase the loss reserves in their balance sheets; these would eventually be used to offset loan losses, as defaulted loans were repaid at less than par. If economic conditions improved sufficiently, and the debtors eventually met their full liabilities, the excess reserves built up by the banks would be released to their shareholders or invested in the expansion of the banks' businesses. Thus a conciliatory default would be like a slow leak in the banks' balance sheets; it could be patched up with profit retentions and reserve additions for long enough to keep the banking system afloat. A repudiation, by contrast, would be like an explosion below decks; it would blow a hole right through the center of the banks' capital structure, which could sink some of the banks before there was even a chance to begin emergency measures.[17]

The attitude of the U.S. government would be equally critical to the preservation of confidence. If the United States recognized the defaulter's economic problems as genuine and adopted a sympathetic attitude, hopes would mount that the conciliatory default could be transformed into a negotiated solution of some kind. Investors in bank stocks would still have cause to fear major losses until the outline of an agreed solution became clear, but any reassurances the authorities offered to depositors might be accepted.

If on the other hand, the U.S. government or even the private sector were to retaliate forcefully against a conciliatory defaulter, the possibility of outright repudiation, accompanied by an outbreak of all-out economic war, could easily smash whatever fragile confidence remained. This does not imply that the United States would have to accept supinely all of a defaulter's demands; a robust initial response might be necessary to force the defaulter back to the bargaining table. But an extended period of economic sanctions, even if it ultimately succeeded in bringing a defaulting country to its knees, could be costly. It would presumably impair even further the defaulter's ability to service debts, and it would require more government support for the banking system than would otherwise be necessary to maintain confidence.

But even if the actions of the defaulter and the authorities were successful in averting a financial panic, political support alone would not be sufficient to preserve confidence indefinitely. A realistic method of accounting for the banks' losses on the defaulted loans would be required. The method chosen for this could be the key to a permanent solution to the debt crisis, for it will also determine how these losses will be shared among bank stockholders, depositors, and the taxpayer.

Capitalization—How Much the Banks Can Afford to Lose

Once it is accepted by the markets and the monetary authorities that losses on defaulted loans can be written off over an extended period, the alarming ratio between the money center banks' exposure to problem borrowers and their capital recedes into the background. The true measure of the impact of default is the proportion of the banks' profits that must be set aside each year for building up reserves against the loans in default.

Even in these terms, the impact of a default would be extremely serious; the interest the money center banks receive each year from the six main problem countries is about 40 percent greater than their total profits in 1983.[18] If this interest stopped being paid, the banks would move immediately into loss. It would then be very difficult for them either to raise new capital or to start building reserves at all for the loans in default. This, in turn, could also thwart the authorities' efforts to prevent a panic among depositors. Once again, conciliatory defaults in which the borrowers continued to pay a modest proportion of their interest in cash and accepted ultimate responsibility for part at least of the rest, would leave the U.S. authorities and the banks with far more room to maneuver.

One plausible way of handling such a conciliatory default would be an accounting device advocated by such current and former bank regulators as Otmar Emminger, former president of the Deutsche Bundesbank, and Anthony Solomon, outgoing president of the New York Federal Reserve Bank.[19] This is the "capitalization" of interest payments: a bank simply adds part of the interest owed by the debtor country to the total of its debts, instead of demanding payment in cash. In effect, capitalization is really an institutionalized and explicit form of the involuntary "new lending" which banks are currently required to undertake. The difference is that under capitalization, banks would be forced to perform this operation year after year, for as long as the capitalization agreement continued.

Part of the interest currently being paid amounts to a form of capital repayment, because inflation currently accounts for a significant proportion of the nominal rate of interest. Suppose, for example, that inflation is running at 5 percent. A bank's exposure to a particular country is then declining in real, inflation-adjusted, dollars by 5 percent a year unless the country borrows more money each year. Thus, part of the "new money" which sovereign borrowers have traditionally raised each year in the capital markets has been tantamount to a refinancing of their existing obligations: this new money was needed simply to pay for the inflationary element in the interest on the borrowers' old debts. If a country with $10 billion of debts in 1984 borrowed $500 million of "new money" during a period when inflation was running at 5 percent, the real value of its debts would be no higher in 1985 than in 1984. Similarly, if a bank with $10 billion of loans to developing countries lent another $500 million, its real exposure would be the same as before. More important, if the bank's capital was also growing at a rate of 5 percent or more, the relationship between its capital and its exposure to developing countries would be constant or declining, despite the "new" lending.

Capitalization locks the banks into maintaining their exposure in real terms. Provided the banks' capital is growing at or above the rate of inflation, capitalization can create an accounting framework for an orderly long-term reduction in the ratio between the banks' sovereign loans and their capital. If the banks capitalize part of their interest, their loan exposures to the problem countries automatically grow at the rate of capitalization. But they can then start setting aside provisions against these exposures out of their reported profits.

According to calculations made by George Salem of A. G. Becker, the nine U.S. money center banks could establish loan loss reserves equal to 4 percent of their problem country exposure if they were prepared to set aside an average of 36 percent of the profits they reported in 1983 (see Table 6.5). Suppose, for the sake of illustration, that a bank with shareholders' capital of $1 billion was owed $1.79 billion by the problem debtors (the ratio of problem loans to capital for the nine money center banks was 179 percent in March 1984).[20] Suppose, further, that 5 percentage points of the interest on the problem loans was capitalized, and that the bank's own capital also grew by 5 percent. Then an annual provision of 4 percent against the problem loans would reduce growth in the banks' total exposure to the problem debtors from 5 percent to 1 percent a year. After ten years the original $1.79 billion of net exposure would have grown to $1.98 billion. But shareholders' capital would have grown to $1.63 billion. Thus, the ratio of problem loans to capital would have improved from 179 percent to 121 percent over the ten years. (The impact of other rates of capitalization and reserving on banks' profits and problem loan exposures is shown in Table 6.5.)

This may seem a disappointing rate of progress in exchange for a near-halving of the money center banks' earnings. But there is an important mitigating factor which is often overlooked. The stock market is *already* discounting up to half of the profits being reported by the money center banks. The price-earnings ratios on which major bank stocks are selling reflect investor disbelief about the profit figures being issued by bank management.[21] In effect, the market is already behaving as if the debtor countries were paying less than their full contractual interest rates—and investors in banks stocks have already sustained very substantial paper losses as a result.

The trouble is that the debtors currently obtain no benefit whatsoever from this implicit interest relief. They go on making payments at their full contractual rates while banks go on adding them to reported profits and investors go on discounting these profits as unsustainable. The combination of capitalization and reserving discussed above *would* reduce the debtors' burden of interest payments on a permanent basis. Accordingly, capitalization could be made part of a permanent negotiated solution to the debt crisis; but it is unlikely to be sufficient to deal with the entire debt problem.

To provide a degree of current interest relief comparable to the maximum potential gain from default—for example, from 12 or 13 percent to 4 or 5 percent—the rate of capitalization would have to be so high that the future solvency of both borrowers and banks would immediately come into question. Capitalization at around the long-term rate of inflation in the U.S. economy—that is, 5 percent—might be realistic;

but forgiveness of interest of 4 or 5 percent on top of this would require either a total abandonment of sound banking practices or a rate of reserving which the present capital of the banks simply could not sustain.[22]

Well before the banks' capital was entirely exhausted, a collapse of confidence would occur. Bank stockholders would lose most, but ultimately others would still have to contribute to the debtors' interest relief: either the losses would fall on creditor country governments, meaning their taxpayers, or on bank depositors if the banks were actually allowed to fail.

Summary

Default could harm the U.S. economy either through a loss of exports or through credit convulsions resulting from banking failures. The loss of exports could be minimized if the government adopted a cooperative, or even a neutral, position toward the defaulter. Managing the banking crisis would be more difficult, but by no means impossible.

Skillful monetary management could in theory avert the dangers of both inflation and deflation, although in practice one or the other would presumably occur to a limited degree. A controlled outcome would only be attainable, though, if confidence in the banking system could be preserved. This would be easier to achieve in the event of a conciliatory default than a repudiation; even then, confidence would be harder to sustain if the U.S. government responded in an aggressive manner than if it attempted to find a cooperative solution.

Even if confidence could be preserved in the short term, the U.S. government would not be able to limit its financial involvement to emergency lending to the banking system. Although money center banks could afford to accept substantial cuts in their reported profits, they do not have the balance sheet strength to provide debtors with the amount of debt relief they might demand in a default. Thus if a default takes place, the U.S. government will have to participate in any permanent resolution, either by helping the debtors directly or by injecting funds through the back door, in the form of capital and support for the banking system.

7
The Politics of Default

In the so-called "realistic" scenario, the debtor countries accept a semi-permanent state of depression. The banks, meantime, continue to pay themselves interest while pushing off amortization into the never-never land of the 21st century. . . . Even if such a situation could be sustained for several years, the result would be a Latin America with no private sector, no middle class and a resentment level ready to explode at any time in the face of our national security.

—Norman Bailey, senior director,
National Security Council, 1981-83,
Latin American Executive Officers Roundtable, February 1984

If the government's efforts to stabilize the domestic economy in the wake of a default proved unsuccessful, political forces demanding retribution against the defaulters would probably prove irresistible, however irrational and self-destructive their demands. But assuming that an immediate economic collapse was averted, the government would be subject to a more elaborate combination of political pressures in determining its response to a default.

First, there would be the reaction of the banks. Many would be tempted to demand retaliation. These calls would be motivated by more than vindictiveness—the banks would wish to deter other borrowers from defaulting. They might also hope that a short burst of sanctions would be sufficient to bring the defaulting country back into line without doing permanent damage to its economy.

It is probable, however, that the big banks most affected by the default might be least vocal in seeking retaliation. They would have more to lose than the smaller banks if a conciliatory default were to turn into an outright repudiation. Sustaining the notion that the default would ultimately be made good could be essential to the big banks' very survival. Several of them also have long-term equity investments to protect in the defaulting country. Thus government actions that embittered diplomatic relations with the defaulting country and weakened its economy would not be in the interests of the big multinational banks. A short episode of retaliation might be attractive if the debtor government appeared to be wavering in its determination to persevere with default. But the political risk that retaliation might incite a much harsher nationalistic line would make this a dangerous gamble.

On balance, the banks might favor retaliation for its deterrent effects if the defaulter was one of the smallest borrowers, such as Chile or the Philippines. But if Mexico or Brazil, the largest debtors, were the first to default, the big banks could find it less costly to try to "buy off" other potential defaulters through financial concessions rather than to promote risky retaliatory measures that were intended to serve as a warning to others. Only if the defaulting government itself seemed unstable or indecisive would retaliation make sense to the big banks.

The calculus for U.S. multinationals with major investments in the defaulting country would be simpler. They would be justifiably frightened of countermeasures against their property in the event of serious aggressive acts by the United States. Historical experience suggests that direct investors would almost certainly suffer costly expropriations at the first signs of economic warfare. In contrast, they would gain nothing from retaliation in support of the bankers' claims.[1] The abstract moral virtues of preserving respect for international contracts would be far outweighed by the danger of expropriations in the minds of industrialists. Hence, publicly the multinationals could be expected to maintain a tactful silence in the event of a default. Privately, they would lobby hard in favor of a speedy negotiated solution that preserved the security of industrial investment in the defaulting country, whatever it meant for bank profits.

There is another reason why direct investors in the defaulting country would probably not demand retribution. They might well be sympathetic to the general aims of the default—to increase the availability of foreign exchange for vital imports needed to promote faster economic growth. Such a strategy, if it succeeded in reviving the defaulter's domestic economy, could be highly beneficial to U.S. direct investors.

The purely domestic business lobbies in the United States would presumably be split between exporters to the defaulting country and domestic industries competing with the defaulter's products. Exporters would want to take advantage of the new opportunities presented by the possible revival in the defaulting country's economy and its capacity to buy foreign goods. Import-competitive industries would, understandably, seize on default as a further pretext for protectionism.

Although the numerical balance of forces between domestic protectionists and potential exporters normally favors the protectionists in trade disputes, this might not be the case if a trade embargo against Latin American countries was at issue. Most U.S. imports—even from the more industrialized Latin-American countries, such as Brazil—are raw materials that do not compete with U.S. production. But American exports to Latin America are primarily manufactured goods or semi-finished goods used by local manufacturing industries. In fact, Latin America is one of the few parts of the world with which the United States normally enjoys a healthy manufacturing export surplus.[2]

Furthermore, a major push for new export markets of the kind that might provoke protectionist sentiment (and has in fact done so, for example, in the case of Chilean copper and Brazilian steel) would not be part of a defaulter's economic strategy. On the contrary, the purpose of default would be to allow the country to increase its imports and divert some of its exports back to domestic consumption. If Brazil or Mexico have recently become a competitive threat to American industries, it is largely because of the pressures imposed on them by their debt problems—their economic structures and trading patterns are not those of South Korea or Taiwan.

For these reasons, a majority of private sector traders, manufacturers, and labor unions might well favor continuing to trade with a defaulter, particularly if the government in question was shrewd enough to announce a program of import expansion and export restraint, to be financed by the proceeds of default.

The interests of domestic economic policymakers must also be considered. Even today, the vast unresolved overhang of sovereign debt is perhaps the biggest single constraint on the ability of the Federal Reserve to pursue its anti-inflationary monetary policy. This constraint has made it equally difficult for the Fed to convince the financial markets that it will stick to this policy, whatever the short-term consequences in terms of higher interest rates.

Until a default actually takes place, central bankers are unlikely to speak out against the present ad hoc rescheduling arrangements. These arrangements, after all, are precarious. Like the emperor's new clothes, they are universally praised by politicians and central bankers; but once they are scorned by a single defaulter, the faith which holds them together will erode overnight. If a major default occurs, the advantages of restructuring sovereign lending on a more stable basis might outweigh the temptation to force a defaulter back into the old system. Policymakers in the administration and the Federal Reserve would undoubtedly wish to bring a defaulter back to the negotiating table; but, if they were rational, they would try to do this by persuasion rather than punishment.

The final, and most important, domestic political constituency is public opinion in general. How likely is it that the American public at large would support political reprisals against Third World countries which defaulted on their debts to the big banks? What if the defaulters were Latin-American nations in the U.S. backyard; if they were attempting to introduce a measure of democracy after decades of military dictatorship; if they were known to be suffering economic crises worse than the depression of the 1930s? And what if, on top of all this, they proclaimed vociferously their support for the rule of law and the free enterprise system; their eager welcome for U.S. direct investment; their willingness to pay their debts as soon as circumstances allowed; and their readiness to continue making small down payments—even in the midst of their economic distress—in order to help preserve the world financial system?

Assuming that the monetary authorities had managed to protect the public from seriously adverse economic consequences directly attributable to the default, it is entirely possible that the public would favor a conciliatory defaulter over the "big banks."

Of course, none of these arguments can prove conclusively that a defaulter will be safe from political retaliation. A dogmatic faith in the efficiency of markets—and of financial markets in particular—combined with a political ideology of strength for its own sake, could easily overwhelm attempts to balance costs against benefits and causes against effects. Nor can the elements of sheer irrationality and simple miscalculation be excluded.

On a more sophisticated level, it would be possible for an American government to try some temporary sanctions against a defaulting country in a short-term attempt to break its will to resist, only to find that its actions had set off an irreversible slide into all-out economic war. It is at least arguable that the behavior of the Reagan administration over the first two years of the debt crisis provides evidence that an amicable response to default cannot be taken for granted. At each stage of the debt crisis, the administration's instinctive reaction has been hostility toward the debtors, tempered by pragmatism only after the dangers of adhering to the ideological hard-line became overwhelmingly plain. The administration's generally unsympathetic response to the debtors' complaints has probably helped to deter default, whether or not this was the deliberate intention. The fact remains, however, that even the Reagan administration has ultimately shown considerable pragmatism when U.S. economic interests have been genuinely endangered—in the original Mexican crisis and subsequently in the congressional resistance to an IMF bill.[3]

Foreign Relations and Default

Whether the U.S. government chose retaliatory action would probably depend, in the end, on foreign policy. In the pre-default phase of the debt crisis, it has been possible for the U.S. government to adopt a passive diplomatic posture. But after a default, the United States would have to make a more explicit choice. Passivity would be a tacit form of cooperation with the defaulter; the alternative would be an active political attack. At present, it is merely disappointing for Latin-American debtors to be refused what they regard as adequate assistance by their U.S. neighbor.

It would, however, provoke an entirely different order of political hostility if the United States were to mount a deliberate assault on the economies of these countries in response to a default.

The often-mentioned political dangers from the current debt-induced economic depression in much of the Third World would be negligible compared with the populist and revolutionary forces which a punitive response to default might unleash. An indication of how seriously one senior policymaker in the State Department views even these milder dangers is provided in the study by Enders (until the summer of 1983, he was assistant secretary of state for inter-American affairs) and Mattione:

> ". . . it is easy to imagine resentment and frustration exploding against governments when they fail to persuade the U.S. and other industrial countries of the need for more generous terms. Not only would the current broad but weak trend towards democracy falter, but public order and national security could also be at risk. And it is worth remembering that after a generation of often failed national security governments, *military intervention may no longer be the plausible alternative it was in the 1960s and 1970s*."[4]

If this analysis is correct, including its thinly veiled suggestion that unrest in the Western Hemisphere could lead to quite different forms of authoritarian rule from the pro-Western military dictatorships of the past two decades, U.S. foreign policy interest becomes obvious. As long as the maintenance of broadly sympathetic regimes in Latin America, the Philippines, and some African countries is a major element in America's geopolitical goals, the domestic pressure for retaliation would have to be powerful before it could be considered a preferable policy to conciliation.[5]

A decision to respond to default with some sort of retaliation is only likely if it appears to be a necessary condition for preserving the banking system and protecting the domestic economy from a precipitous decline. But, given that retaliation would actually aggravate—rather than avert—a banking and economic crisis, the diplomatic arguments against retaliation would probably be decisive.[6]

Default and the Rule of Law

Yet there is still another argument in favor of a decisive U.S. reaction against default. This is the case for defending the "rule of law" and the dominant role of private markets in international economic relations. Without an unmistakable commitment by the world's most powerful capitalist country to support the rights of private creditors, the fear is that international market mechanisms could begin to erode, and governments could take ever-greater liberties with the property of foreign investors. Both trade and international investment could thereby suffer in the long run.

This is a powerful argument for a clearcut policy of some kind by the U.S. government, not only in the event of a default but even in the current phase of the debt crisis. It does not, however, establish a need to retaliate against an economically justified default. Even though the U.S. government would undoubtedly recognize a duty to assist international investors against unreasonable and discriminatory attacks by foreign countries, it is under no obligation to protect them unconditionally from the consequences of their own unwise business decisions.[7]

This position is one which governments have frequently taken in past defaults. As in earlier episodes of widespread sovereign default during the past two centuries, lenders have contributed to the current problems through excessive lending and inadequate examination of the economic circumstances of borrowing countries. The potential weakness of legal sanctions against a sovereign borrower should have been familiar to the banks when they made their loans. There appears to be no moral reason why the United States would choose either to assist or obstruct them in attempting to recover their investments. The U.S. government's only moral obligation would be to press for a return to the negotiating table after a default had occurred, but it would wish to do so in any event in the interests of domestic monetary stability (see Chapter 6).

The whole framework for these post-default negotiations would be very different from the current ad hoc and semi-voluntary rescheduling arrangements. The primary aim of the present reschedulings has been to protect the solvency of the banks. But defaulters would insist on shifting the focus to their domestic growth prospects. The main constraint on such negotiations would not be the maximum concessions that the banks could afford, but the maximum burdens that the debtors could bear. The amount of debt relief that such a shift in the bargaining perspective would bring about would inevitably lead to the financial involvement of the United States and other creditor governments. The ensuing three-cornered negotiation between bankers, debtors, and creditor governments might aptly be called an "agreed default." Whether this was seen as a sensible and pragmatic resolution of a chronic malaise in the world economic system or as an abrogation of free market principles and the rule of law would depend, in large part, on how creditor governments presented it. This in turn might revolve around the sort of economic and political conditions which the borrowers were persuaded to accept in exchange for debt relief.

The IMF and Economic Adjustment

America's diplomatic response to the debt crisis has so far consisted mainly of praise for the IMF adjustment process, and insistence that the way forward for debtor countries lies through policy changes, rather than new financing. The policymakers show little sign so far of being able to distinguish between the short-run necessity of IMF programs and their unsuitability as permanent solutions to the economic problems of the debtor countries. Although IMF-type adjustment policies have helped to reestablish economic equilibrium in many of the debtor countries, they may work in the long run against U.S. global interests.

First, the institutional philosophy of the IMF could jeopardize U.S. efforts to liberalize the international trading system. The IMF has taken on an entirely new—and highly constructive—role since 1982 in marshalling resources from the private banks, but the main thrust of any IMF program is still to minimize the adjusting country's need for external financing. This means generating huge trade surpluses, which threaten to destabilize the international trading system. Brazil's trade surplus, for example, will have to be equal to between 40 and 50 percent of its total merchandise imports in each of the next ten years if it is to maintain the rate of debt servicing likely to be expected of it.

Such huge *and permanent* trade surpluses are unprecedented in economic history, and risk provoking protectionism on a globally damaging scale. Even Japan has never run trade surpluses of this magnitude for such extended periods.[8] Developing countries such as Korea and Singapore, which have been the main victims of protectionist forces in America and Europe in the past, have actually imported more from the industrialized world than they exported, conferring employment benefits on industrialized countries, which have helped to counterbalance the protectionist lobbies. Such counterpressures will be much weaker against the protectionists who demand barriers to Mexican and Brazilian exports and can point out that the debtors' record surpluses are being achieved through blatantly discriminatory import controls and export subsidies.

It is quite likely, therefore, that Latin-American adjustment programs, if maintained much longer, will give a further boost to worldwide protectionist sentiment. The idea that the debt crisis could be resolved by a *reduction* in international protectionism assumes an altogether unrealistic forbearance on the part of American and European industrial lobbies in the face of the open trade manipulation that the Third World debtors have been forced to undertake. Far from eliminating the international economic distortions caused by the financial blunders of the 1970s, the IMF's present adjustment philosophy simply transfers the distortions from world capital markets to world trade.

A second caveat about the role of the IMF is an inevitable corollary of the current approach to rescheduling: international capital flows to developing countries will be allocated for years or even decades largely through IMF-related programs.[9] It is hard to see why U.S. political leaders regard this massive centralization of international economic decision-making as furthering U.S. free-market goals.

In the short term, of course, the IMF's policies may strengthen market forces *within* some developing countries. The semi-voluntary rescheduling agreements between the IMF and the banks may also sustain the illusion that international capital is still being allocated in a market-oriented, nonpolitical manner. In the longer run, though, the prospect that the IMF will emerge as a permanent regulator both of international capital flows and of domestic economic policies in developing countries will turn it into precisely the sort of institution of economic "world government" that the conservative current in U.S. foreign policy has always feared and opposed.[10]

Another argument against the plenipotentiary role of the IMF is more familiar. The IMF has acted as a focus for nationalistic, and ultimately, anti-American political agitation in many countries. Enders and Mattione suggest how this could be disastrous to U.S. interests if the IMF's emergency treatment is mistakenly taken to be a permanent cure by either the creditor or debtor governments:

> In most countries, stabilization plans have been sold as short, necessary operations, soon to result in a new burst of growth. In some they are being instituted by technicians without broad political consent. When the crisis in some countries drags on with per capita incomes below 1980 levels, as they may be for much of this decade, and without credible promise of relief,

it is easy to imagine resentment and frustration exploding and turning against governments when they fail to persuade the U.S. and other industrialized countries of the need for more generous terms. . . . [The rest of this passage is quoted on page 55.][11]

Paradoxically, all of these criticisms of the IMF are much more cogent when viewed from the creditors' than the debtors' perspective. The debtors have little cause to complain about the general thrust of the IMF's economic philosophy. The IMF is pushing the debtors' policies in a general direction that should be conducive to democracy and, eventually, economic progress. The only trouble is that the present burden of debt servicing dictates a rate of political progress and economic growth that is unacceptably slow. Some debtor countries could decide that the political progress which they have now begun to make, partly as an indirect result of the debt crisis, would be consolidated further through default.

Development Models and Default

While there are many reasons for the debt crisis, the domestic economic policies pursued by the debtors themselves have been the single most important cause. If the governments of Mexico, Brazil, Argentina, Chile, the Philippines, Nigeria, and many other countries had not adopted credit-driven models of economic development that relied on foreign borrowing to maintain excessive consumption levels and overvalued exchange rates, their countries would not today be mortgaged to the banks. Of course, the debtors' policies were aided and abetted by the short-sightedness of international bankers; and they were in several cases actively encouraged and lavishly praised by politicians and economists from industrialized countries.[12] But some developing countries managed to resist the temptations held out by the international banks and the economic fads of the 1970s. Specifically, these countries avoided the two errors that nearly every IMF adjustment program is now striving to correct: excessive public sector deficits and overvalued exchange rates.

These misguided policies are now being reversed in one debtor country after another; and looking back from the twenty-first century, the debt crisis could conceivably turn out to have been the start of a new and constructive era in the histories of most of the developing countries. As the IMF stated in its 1984 *World Economic Outlook,* the debtors' new policies "could play an important role in the long-term process of shifting a broad range of the world's manufacturing activities to developing countries."[13]

In a conciliatory default, the thrust of policy adjustment would not be entirely reversed. A conciliatory defaulter would have to maintain some interest payments to private creditors, albeit at a reduced rate, and would probably maintain full servicing on debts to public institutions like the IMF and World Bank. Creditor country governments might well set policy conditions in return for acquiescing to an "agreed default." Most important, the opening up of the debtor countries' economies over the past ten to fifteen years has set in train an irreversible change in consumer expectations. This will make it politically impossible for the debtor countries to return permanently to a policy of unmitigated protectionism and import substitution. Even the poorest Brazilians, Chileans, and Nigerians expect to be able to buy foreign goods sometime in their lives.

Many debtor countries now recognize the need to move in the general direction advocated by the IMF. Mexico's Finance Minister Jesus Silva Herzog, for example, insists that Mexico's economic adjustment was drawn up by the Mexican government and would have been adhered to whether or not there was an IMF program. Politicians who advocate default are not necessarily seeking a return to the policies of inward looking import substitution of the 1950s. This does not mean, however, that the rate of adjustment required by IMF programs, still less the principle of long-term IMF control over economic decisionmaking, has been accepted.

Apart from the nationalistic resentment about the IMF's role, there is also a strong intellectual case that can be made against the speed of adjustments demanded by the IMF. Less-developed economies, with their imperfect markets, their shortages of capital, their weak infrastructure, and their inadequate resources of trained manpower, are likely to respond quite slowly and inefficiently to policy changes such as agricultural price improvements and currency devaluation. Policies that have worked smoothly and rapidly in industrialized countries such as Britain and Italy can hardly be expected to be as effective and painless in Mexico or Nigeria.

From this standpoint, a major purpose of any rational default strategy would be to provide the debtor economy with sufficient foreign exchange resources to spread the effort of adjustment to the new economic model over a period of five or ten years and to enable a resumption of economic growth. The IMF in its public pronouncements argues against such a stretching of adjustment on the ground that it would reduce a nation's will to reform.[14] But many other IMF officials (and almost all of their counterparts at the World Bank) concede privately that there is only one real rationale for the rapid rate of adjustment currently demanded. This is the impossibility, under current rescheduling arrangements, of marshalling sufficient resources to finance a more leisurely rate of deficit reduction and policy reform. A strategy of conciliatory default would be designed to achieve just this.

In the negotiations that followed the declaration of a conciliatory default, it could turn out that the differences between the creditor and debtor governments were not so much over matters of principle as of degree. Domestic policy issues such as the gradual lowering of protectionist barriers, the encouragement of foreign direct investment, and even the development of a continuous advisory relationship with the IMF and World Bank would not be ruled out by a rational defaulting country that was attempting to assure a cooperative reception from the United States and other creditor governments.

8

The Likelihood of Default

There has been some recovery in industrial countries, especially in the United States. However, there are already signs pointing to the end of that springboard. . . . Protectionism grows and continues to frustrate our possibilities for access to the industrial countries. Many of the adjustment programs negotiated with the IMF have been revised because they proved inadequate. Some of them have left sad balances of death and public unrest. . . .

All of this makes it necessary to revise the basic criteria by which the problem of our countries' foreign debt is examined. Therefore, the presence of our governments here reflects a situation that we have not created but that neither we nor anyone can conceal any longer: the foreign debt problem has stopped being a simple financial problem and is now undoubtedly an international political issue. . . .

—Belisario Betancur, president of Colombia
Cartagena Debtors' Conference, June 23, 1984

The evidence examined in the paper suggests that a rational borrower is unlikely to decide on a total repudiation of debts. Repudiation has no advantages and many disadvantages in comparison to less provocative and more equivocal forms of default.

A formal "debtors' cartel" is equally implausible. This is not so much because countries with divergent interests and economic prospects would be unable to agree on a coordinated position. Because a debtor's cartel does not need to include all developing countries, it is quite possible that a subgroup would be able to unite. The main objection to a debtor's cartel is the same as the one against flagrant repudiation; it would needlessly provoke governmental and public opinion in creditor countries. A further danger for the potential defaulters is that simultaneous default by numerous borrowers would make it that much harder for the monetary authorities to stabilize their banking systems, and would thus increase the probability of a serious economic downturn. Such a downturn would rebound on the defaulters both through its direct economic effects and through the vindictive political emotions it might arouse in the creditor countries. Nevertheless, a debtors' cartel, in the sense of a simultaneous default by several borrowers, cannot be ruled out quite as categorically as an outright repudiation. It could have one advantage for the potential defaulters; it would eliminate one of the few rational arguments in favor of retaliation by creditor governments and banks, namely, the hope that retaliation against the first defaulter would have a deterrent effect on others.

Much more likely than a flagrant repudiation or a debtors' cartel is some form of conciliatory default by one or more borrowers, acting independently in a formal sense, but perhaps with a degree of coordination behind the scenes.

It may be argued that defaults, in this sense, have already been committed by most of the debtor countries. The moratorium on debt repayments declared by Mexico on August 23, 1982, could have been interpreted as a default, as could the buildup of $3 billion in interest arrears by Argentina in 1984, and similar actions by other debtors from Peru to the Philippines. These actions have not been generally described as defaults partly because default is in the eye of the beholder, and creditors found it tactically inopportune in each of these cases to term the borrowers formally "in default." More important, the moratoria announced in the first phase of the debt crisis were considered by creditors and debtors alike to be strictly temporary arrangements, paving the way for cooperative debt reschedulings.

In the next phase of the debt crisis, it may be harder for creditors to be so liberal in their interpretations. If, for example, a debtor country unilaterally declares that it will in the future pay interest of only 3 percent on all its medium-term bank debts and will pay no principal for thirty years, there can be no question that such an act is a default. Whether bankers decide to call it that immediately would be a tactical matter; but either way, such an action by a major debtor would create shock waves in the international financial community.

A default, in this broad sense of the word, appears quite likely in the foreseeable future.

Economic conditions in much of Latin America still show insufficient signs of broadly based improvement. Forecasts based on reasonable assumptions about interest rates and the world economy suggest that the shortage of foreign currency will be the biggest constraint preventing countries from resuming growth, controlling inflation, and raising their living standards significantly during the rest of the decade. Banks will not voluntarily, or even under the present semivoluntary negotiated arrangements, provide the additional financial resources which some of these countries require to start growing again, and there is no sign that industrialized country governments are prepared to make good the short-fall in foreign financing, either directly or through multilateral agencies like the IMF and World Bank.

The short-term opportunities for relieving the foreign exchange constraint through trade are also near exhaustion. In fact, the trade surpluses generated by some of the debtor countries are already too large for the health of the international free trade system. An increase in foreign direct investment would certainly be useful and should be promoted, but capital inflows from this source will always remain modest relative to the magnitude of debt servicing. They are unlikely to revive at all until the constraint on domestic economic growth of the debtor countries is lifted. Thus default for some debtor governments will be the only way to relieve the foreign exchange pressures which they believe to be their main impediments to economic and social progress.

On the other side of the balance sheet, a less familiar factor makes some defaults plausible within the next few years: the penalties for a *conciliatory* default may not be as daunting as is often supposed. On the contrary, these penalties could be surprisingly moderate. The remedies available to the private creditors themselves are of limited use. A bank attempting to invoke the modest legal sanctions available might do more harm to itself than to the defaulter. There would be little solidarity between banks and other private economic creditors, such as multinational corporations. And creditor country governments *should* be able to contain the impact of a default on their domestic economies, so that the political demands for an aggressive response out of vindictiveness would be small. What is more, a rational balancing of the costs and benefits of retaliation by the creditor countries will suggest that a degree of cooperation with the defaulter would be more advantageous than aggression.

Nevertheless, the inherent uncertainties in all these arguments—plus the possibility of a miscalculation or irrationality in one or more creditor countries—imply that debtors will remain extremely fearful of retaliation. Accordingly, default is unlikely to be an active option until debtor countries have consolidated their domestic political systems and assured themselves of strong popular support, including a willingness to accept further sacrifices, if necessary, in the name of national self-determination; until they have built up foreign exchange reserves and shifted enough of their trade onto a cash or barter basis to be able to survive the possible withdrawal of trade credit; and until they have carried out some of the most painful adjustments which would have been required in any case to correct the imbalances in their domestic economies.

Mexico and Argentina are already reaching the point where these conditions are partly satisfied. Brazil will probably do so by the spring of 1985, after a new president is inaugurated. However, Mexico may have less incentive to default than some other countries. As an oil exporter, its long-term economic and financial prospects look less gloomy than those of most other Latin-American countries.

Argentina would be in the strongest position to cope with possible retaliation from creditors. Nevertheless, it may be fearful of being the first country to default openly, if only because the magnitude of its debts is not quite big enough to guarantee catastrophic damage to the world financial system if creditor nations decided to risk subjecting it to an economic siege. Thus, Argentina could conceivably be punished for default as a deterrent to other debtor countries, although such action is by no means likely. For Argentina, an attractive tactic might be "tacit default"—failure to fulfill its obligations without actually announcing this as a policy.

Brazil would be more likely to default openly. The weight of its loans in all the major banks' balance sheets is so great that the uncertainty surrounding an extended period of tacit default would be unacceptable to bankers and creditor governments alike. The country would be called into account for its arrears within a year at most. But, economic war against Brazil could be a disastrous policy for banks, multinational corporations, and U.S. foreign policy interests. Thus, an open, but highly conciliatory default by Brazil is plausible. It might involve some of the following features:

Brazil would present its actions as a reluctant and unavoidable response to overwhelming economic problems. It would not deny its ultimate responsibility for its debts or declare a temporary moratorium on all of them. Debts to other governments and to international institutions such as the IMF and World Bank would continue to be serviced in full, as might a large proportion of the trade credits. Brazil might even stress that the foreign exchange it saved through default would be used to boost imports from the United States and other industrialized countries, to ease economic constraints on foreign multinationals, and to cut back on protectionist export subsidies.

The banks would probably be offered a *unilateral* rescheduling formula. This might involve a major lengthening of maturities; substantial capitalization of interest; and a demand for some of the interest to be forgiven altogether. Such an attempt to impose a unilateral rescheduling would not be the borrowers' last word on the subject

Although unilaterally imposed, the terms of the offer could hardly be nonnegotiable, if the defaulter wanted to preserve its conciliatory image.

In effect, such a default would be a call for a new round of long-term debt negotiations between the borrower, the banks, and the creditor governments (acting perhaps through the IMF or other international institutions). The critical difference between postdefault negotiations and the current semivoluntary rescheduling would be that the framework for bargaining would be set by the demands of the debtor, not by the needs of the banks. By the act of default, the borrowing country would have asserted that it was prepared to override the constraints imposed even by the banks' solvency requirements.

A Search for Agreed Default

Assuming that an ultimate bargaining position existed that would be less than disastrous to all three parties—the borrowers, the bankers, and the creditor governments—it would be possible in theory for a solution to be reached without the disruption of a default. In reality, however, an immediate leap from the current ad hoc reschedulings, based on market interest rates and traditional banking arrangements, to such an "agreed default" is not very plausible.

The banks themselves are unlikely to propose it, in part because many of them do not accept that default is a realistic threat. There are also other reasons why banks would be unlikely to take the initiative. Whatever concessions they offered, the banks would expect the borrowers automatically to demand more. Bank managements that volunteered to accept losses could expect attacks from their shareholders. In addition, banks that took the initiative in offering concessions would almost certainly forfeit the chance of pleading successfully later for government financial support.

In principle, creditor governments could take the initiative away from the potential defaulters. Such a move would certainly be preferable to any action by the debtors. A concessionary debt restructuring proposed by creditor governments would be much less likely to precipitate a financial panic than even the mildest form of conciliatory default by the debtors. Indeed, an "agreed default" arranged by creditor governments might well be hailed as a triumphant resolution of the debt crisis, even though an identical arrangement imposed by the debtors could lead to a collapse of financial confidence.

Like the bankers, though, creditor governments appear to feel at present that any offer of help on their part would automatically expose them to unconscionable further demands from the other parties in the bargain—the debtors and bankers. It is probable, therefore, that debtors will have to take the law into their own hands if they want any substantial relief from their present financial constraints.

But supposing that creditor governments did take the threat of default seriously. Would there be anything they could—or should—do about it?

Options for Government Action

Three broad types of policies are available to the United States and other creditor governments: to do nothing, to strengthen the banks, or to help the debtors.

The U.S. administration's view that debt problems are a "private" matter between bankers, debtors, and the IMF has been aptly described as "a joke" by one Latin-American finance minister.[1] Nonintervention *is* a form of government action in the context of the present debt crisis. The U.S. government's noninvolvement, moreover, is disingenuous. The IMF, after all, is heavily influenced in its policies by the U.S. Treasury. The IMF's resources, its policies on adjustment, and lately, even its senior personnel appointments,[2] have been determined largely by the U.S. government. There is little doubt, for example, that the other industrialized countries which nominally share control over the IMF would support substantial quota increases, or modifications in the balance between adjustment and financing, if the Reagan administration endorsed these ideas. The current dependence of the IMF on U.S. government policy is one reason why the debtor countries are increasingly making their appeals for policy changes directly to the U.S. government, rather than to the IMF itself.

The second reason for considering "hands off" to be a positive policy response is that the government will inevitably become involved in rescue operations if the present rescheduling arrangements prove unsustainable and lead to a default.

In the event of default, creditor country governments would have to support their banking systems, and the help required would almost certainly need to go beyond "lender of last resort" liquidity injections from central banks. Major U.S. commercial banks would be threatened with insolvency as well as illiquidity under current banking regulations if either Mexico or Brazil or a combination of other smaller debtors defaulted. To prevent a disastrous financial collapse, the U.S. government would either have to relax the prudential capital requirements in current banking regulations or inject substantial new capital into the banking system. It would probably do both. Nevertheless, a chain of defaults by numerous big borrowers could wipe out so much of the U.S. banks' current capital that a major part of the U.S. banking system might need, in effect, to be temporarily nationalized. The banks would be denationalized eventually, but only after new repayment programs were agreed with the debtors. Even then, the government could be forced to remove some or all of the defaulted loans from the banks' balance sheets to speed a return to the private sector.

The collapse of confidence in financial markets and in the economy generally while these rescue operations were being organized would be a high price to pay simply for preserving the illusion of non-intervention. The present insouciance of the creditor governments can only be justified by two assumptions, which are to some degree contradictory: that default is extremely unlikely, and that any action taken to prepare for a default would risk bringing one about.

Strengthening the Banking System

If the U.S. government recognized the danger of a default, it could take various steps immediately to increase the banking system's resilience. The major international banks could be forced to strengthen their capital positions further by seeking new equity or long-term finance, by withholding dividend payments, by setting up larger reserves for loan losses, and by reining in their acquisition of new assets.[3] Unfortunately, several of these actions would tend to counteract each other. Stopping dividend payments, for example, would make it more difficult to raise new equity. Cutting back on the growth of new lending would prevent the international banks from diversifying their loan portfolios away from sovereign loans and might reduce the domestic profits available to offset loan losses. Establishing larger loan loss reserves would reduce the banks' reported profits (although it would have no effect on their cash flows), again making capital-raising operations harder.

Despite these apparent contradictions, there is much that banks could do, or be forced to do, to strengthen their balance sheets. The arguments for enlarging loan loss reserves and cutting dividend payments are particularly telling. Investors are *already* treating bank stocks as if their earnings and dividends were substantially lower than the figures they are reporting: continuing to publish unrealistic profits and to pay out dividends which could prove unsustainable fools no one and does not assist the banks in raising new capital.

Such precautionary strengthening of the banking system has already been carried out in several major creditor countries, including Germany, Switzerland, Sweden, and Japan.[4] But these moves do nothing directly to help the debtor countries or to avert the possibility of default. It is even possible that by making the banking system more robust, such measures could make default more likely. The danger of inadvertently triggering a global economic catastrophe is one of the biggest deterrents for a rational defaulter.

Indirectly, a strengthening of bank capital could nevertheless be helpful to the debtors, since it would enable banks to offer interest concessions which they otherwise could not afford. Once a bank has established reserves of 33 percent against its lending to Argentina, for example, it can afford to forgive Argentina one-third of its debt or to reduce the country's interest payments by one-third, without incurring further loss. Similarly, if the bank's capital has been doubled, temporary losses resulting from interest concessions or loan write-offs are less likely to bring insolvency.

Some German, Swiss, and Japanese bankers believe that they have already built up the capital and reserve strength to participate in plausible debt restructuring or "agreed default" schemes without incurring further serious losses. Because of their exiguous bank reporting requirements, it is impossible to say whether or not this is true. What can be asserted with confidence is that the capital ratios of U.S. banks are likely to remain so weak for the foreseeable future that any large concessions to the debtor countries would put their solvency at risk.

The U.S. government could nonetheless urge or force the banks to subsidize the borrowers beyond the prudent limits imposed by their present capital ratios by, for example, requiring banks to "cap" interest rates.[5] But it could do this only if the Fed and the Treasury were prepared to guarantee the solvency of the banks and provide them with additional capital as required.

If the U.S. government took this approach, it would in effect be aiding the debtor countries through the back door of the banking system. Given the alternative of offering relief directly to the debtors, either through the IMF and World Bank or on a bilateral basis, it is questionable whether this kind of assistance would be sensible.

Politically, the nationalization of banks, even on a temporary basis, would be difficult, if not impossible. Economically, a more transparent form of government assistance, which went directly to the roots of the problem by relieving the debtors of part of their interest burden, would produce fewer distortions in the financial markets. The direct approach would also help to strengthen the ties between debtor and creditor countries, offer the possibility of influencing the debtors' economic policies, and speed the resumption of economic growth.

Helping the Debtors

The simplest method of averting default would be to provide the debtors with substantial new finance. One of the most widely discussed proposals is for a special IMF facility available to all borrowers during periods of unusually high real interest rates and repayable if and when real interest rates fell below "normal" levels, for example, below 3 percent.[6] Alternatively, there could be a new allocation of Special Drawing Rights (SDR), which would provide controlled amounts of free liquidity to all IMF members. Of these ideas, an SDR allocation would have two major advantages over a new IMF facility: it would not need to be financed by IMF member governments, since allocation of SDRs is the IMF's equivalent of "printing money"; and enlarged SDR holdings would not increase even further the developing countries' burden of debt.[7]

The World Bank is another possible vehicle for substantial new official lending to the debtor countries. The Bank's "structural adjustment loan" program, which carries with it conditions widely regarded as more conducive than the IMF's to long-term growth, could be greatly increased if additional funds were made available. An advantage of World Bank financing is that the Bank, unlike the Fund, borrows most of its resources from the international capital markets. Member governments provide capital subscriptions which are in effect guarantees, with only a low proportion of the capital (currently 7.5 percent) actually paid in. The Bank could thus be a means of reintermediating between the excess liquidity which has been building up in international money markets and the borrowing needs of the developing countries. The main drawback of Bank financing is that it would need to carry market interest rates, and would therefore continue to add to the burden of developing countries' debts.

The most obvious source of additional lending is the private banking system. Although the banks are no longer willing to refinance more than a small proportion of the debtor countries' interest payments on a voluntary basis, by a combination of moral suasion, regulatory pressure, and if necessary, legislation, creditor governments could force their banks to lend as much new money as they considered appropriate.

The simplest and most rational way of expanding bank lending on a long-term basis would be to encourage banks and debtors to capitalize part of the interest on their loans. This would ensure that all banks involved in each country shared equally in the new loans: each bank's new lending would be directly proportional to its existing exposure. The main constraint on such forced drafts on private bank financing would be the need to allow the banks gradually to improve their prudential ratios by diversifying away from potentially insolvent sovereign borrowers. The calculations presented earlier[8] suggest that capitalization at around the underlying rate of U.S. inflation, say 5 percent a year, accompanied by the establishment of significant loan loss reserves, would be compatible with a gradual reduction in banks' relative exposure to the developing countries. A much higher rate of capitalization could cast doubt on some banks' long-term solvency.

A final way of giving developing countries access to additional sources of foreign exchange is through trade. Dismantling protectionist barriers to developing countries' imports could probably make a modest contribution to averting default. But the revenues from higher developing countries' exports are less likely to be spent on debt servicing than on higher imports. This would be a desirable end in itself, but not a way out of the debt crisis.

None of these options, taken individually, would be capable of offering as much debt relief as the major borrowers could hope to obtain by defaulting. But by combining forced lending from private banks with capital injections for the U.S. banking system and modest amounts of official assistance directly to the borrowers, a package capable of averting default and improving dramatically the debtor countries' economic outlook can readily be designed. The Bank of England has prepared for its internal use a list of about 100 schemes that have been mooted over the past two years for "solving" the debt crisis. Given the will, there clearly would be no shortage of ideas for dealing with the debt crisis in a controlled and rational manner—either before or after a default. Only two elements are lacking before this chronic malignancy in the international financial system can be cured. These elements, both critical, are realism and money.

The only way to arrive at the view, so popular at present among bankers and Western politicians, that "there is no alternative" to the present ad hoc rescheduling arrangements is to insist in advance that any alternative would have to maintain the present level of bank profits, cost the creditor countries nothing, and leave the debtor countries better off. Obviously, such a solution, which imposes no costs on anyone, may not exist. But the realistic prospect of default implies that some or all of the parties involved in the debt crisis may be forced to bear extra costs anyway—whether or not they agree in advance.

Toward a Cooperative Solution

Without offering a specific prescription, it is possible to identify some of the criteria which any negotiated solution to the debt crisis would ideally satisfy.

A negotiated solution to the debt crisis would have two broad objectives. In order to be acceptable to the potential defaulters, it would have to reduce the resource transfer out of these countries to a level compatible with an early return to a relatively rapid rate of per capita growth. To be acceptable to the creditor governments, it would have to protect the world banking system from collapse and preserve a modicum of respect for private property in international commercial relations.

Important subsidiary objectives for the creditor governments would be to achieve these goals at a minimum cost to their taxpayers, to avoid an excessive extension of worldwide economic regulation, and to improve the economic management of developing countries so as to promote world trade, private enterprise, and economic growth.

These objectives could be met by a restructuring based on the following principles:

- The restructuring should avoid subsidizing countries which would be able and willing to continue servicing their loans under existing arrangements. This means that negotiations should continue to be done on a case-by-case basis, without lumping all developing countries into some new global institution. It also requires that countries which request special treatment should be made to bear a cost of some kind. Since by definition these countries would be incapable of bearing economic penalties, the costs for requesting special debt restructuring would have to be political in nature, involving close monitoring of their economies. Countries which agreed to abide by present nonconcessionary arrangements could also be offered incentives less costly than the subsidies provided for those who requested special treatment.

- The alternative arrangements should preferably involve no new international institutions or global negotiations. These would be difficult to organize in a moment of crisis and might open the creditor countries to all kinds of unacceptable political demands from the developing world.

- The restructuring should make it possible for both borrowers and bankers to predict clearly and plan for their long-term costs and obligations.

• The restructuring should not only reestablish economic growth in debtor nations, but should aim to reintegrate the countries into an orderly system of free trade. They should involve a lowering of protectionist barriers by both industrialized countries and borrowers.

• Banks would have to acknowledge substantial losses, but these losses would need to be limited and spread over an extended period so as to preserve the integrity of the banking system. Once lending was reorganized, there would be more certainty about the level of future debt service. This would improve the quality of bank earnings and might limit the fall in bank stock prices.

• Creditor governments would have to bear the excess long-term costs of the restructurings, beyond the write-offs that could be tolerated by the banking system. This could be done through the World Bank or the IMF and should preferably involve guarantees, rather than cash contributions. Governments might also have to inject funds into their banking systems on a short-term basis to preserve confidence; but adequate assistance to the debtors would limit the necessity for this kind of aid to the creditors.

• Countries which applied for special treatment would be forced to submit to substantial outside supervision of their economic and financial policies. This supervision might include a requirement for them to open their economies to more foreign equity investment. These adjustment policies would be of a more detailed micro-economic nature than those currently imposed by the IMF. They might have similar macro-economic objectives, such as the reduction of government deficits and the devaluation of exchange rates, but they would allow the borrowers a longer adjustment process than at present. For the debtor countries, the political costs of accepting conditions would be substantial. They would be high enough to deter countries from requesting special treatment unless they really needed it. But they would be less unpleasant than the probable costs of repudiation (which would be the only type of default available to a debtor government which rejected on political grounds a reasonable restructuring proposal offering substantial debt relief).

A solution satisfying all of these criteria is quite conceivable. In practice, it is likely to be imposed by one or more of the debtors in something like the following manner:

The debtor country would announce a unilateral rescheduling in which it simply offered to pay the banks a "normal" real interest rate—

of, say, 3 percent—in cash. It would turn part of its remaining interest obligations into new long-term loans and demand relief from the rest. All principal repayments would be stretched out to twenty years or more.

Creditor governments might respond to such a default with a counteroffer along the following lines:

Suppose the contractual interest rate was 13 percent. The debtor country would be allowed to capitalize part of its interest at a rate no higher than inflation, say, 5 percent. It would be required to pay a real interest rate of 4 percent in cash. The banks would be forced to forgive a further 2 percent of the interest; banks which refused to do so would be given no government assistance in pursuing legal sanctions against the defaulter and would forfeit government support for their uninsured depositors. This would leave 2 percent of interest uncovered; the creditor governments would agree to finance this through the World Bank on condition that the borrower agreed to a long-term program of economic adjustment and financial recuperation administered jointly by the World Bank and IMF. If the defaulting country agreed to such a program, it also would be guaranteed access to industrialized country markets and export credits, but would be expected to submit to a degree of external supervision roughly in proportion to the amount of interest it was seeking to capitalize.

Banks would be allowed to take some of the accrued but unpaid interest into income, but would be required to start establishing substantial loan loss reserves with part of the accruing interest. This would give them a strong incentive to offer much better terms than at present to countries which were prepared not to request special treatment.

Such borrowers could also be offered additional incentives for staying within the semivoluntary framework, for example, by having their present IMF conditionality relaxed, their access to industrialized country markets expanded, or the availability of export credits guaranteed.

What would be the costs and benefits of such a scheme? Rough orders of magnitude can be readily calculated.

The big U.S. banks would lose about half their current reported profits. In exchange, their exposure to "problem" debtors would be reduced, slowly but steadily, from 179 percent of capital to 100 percent or less.[9]

For borrowers, the steady growth in the debt burden, which would amount to 2 percent a year in real terms, would be easily sustainable, if their economies could return to growth trends, say, of 5 percent a year in real terms.[10] For Brazil, Mexico, Venezuela, and Argentina, the temptation to default would be dramatically reduced (see Table 8.1).

For the governments of creditor countries, the combined annual cost, even if every Third World borrower demanded special treatment, would be about $6 billion, if they lent to the debtor countries directly, or around $500 million in paid-in capital contributions, if the lending was done on a leveraged basis by the World Bank.[11]

Any such solution might fall well short of perfection. Some banks would find ways of wriggling out of their exposure, leaving others to shoulder a bigger burden. A few banks might become insolvent. Some borrowers might still default, because they rejected the principle of externally imposed economic policies or because they refused to make any net transfers at all to the industrialized countries. Some politicians in the United States and Europe might prefer protectionism and retaliation to cooperation, or they might balk at providing any help at all to feckless debtors and bankers.

But for the rational majority, this scheme and dozens of others like it illustrate that an all-out trade war or a decade of economic slump are not the only possible outcomes of the debt crisis.

Human ingenuity, with political will, is equal to the task of finding better solutions.

Notes

Chapter 1

1. Japan's trade surplus in 1984 is expected to be $30 billion, or 2.3 percent of GNP; Brazil's likely $12 billion surplus is 5.6 percent of GNP; and Mexico's $12 billion surplus is 9.4 percent of GNP. Between 1983 and 1992, Brazil's trade surpluses are forecast to average about 4 percent of GNP, and Mexico's about 7 percent, against a likely 1.5 percent of GNP in Japan. See Table 1.2 for source.

2. Merchandise imports in the six major Latin-American economies (Argentina, Brazil, Colombia, Chile, Mexico, and Venezuela) fell by 44 percent from 1981 to 1984. Adjusted for dollar inflation, Latin America's imports will, on current trends, remain below their 1981 peaks until well into the 1990s. Thus the outside world will have to accept a sharp and quasi-permanent deterioration in its merchandise trade balance with Latin America, without erecting new protectionist barriers. See Table 1.2 for source.

3. The decline in the U.S. growth rate which is now widely expected is particularly serious. The U.S. boom was responsible for almost the whole of Latin America's export "miracle"—85 percent of the increase in Latin America's exports from mid-1982 to mid-1984 went to the United States. A further 8 percent went to Japan and the Far East, where the faster-than-expected expansion was also attributable to the U.S. economy's performance. Thus, to a large extent, Latin America's export surplus is the counterpart of a massive U.S. trade deficit which is widely regarded as unsustainable in the long run. Indeed, some bankers have begun to warn against any abrupt correction in the U.S. deficit for precisely this reason. See Morgan Guaranty Trust, *World Financial Markets,* October/November 1984, pp. 10-11.

4. See Anatole Kaletsky, "When the Debtors Said No," *Financial Times,* December 28, 1984. For a more detailed history of sovereign defaults, see William Wynne, *State Insolvency and Foreign Bondholders: Case Histories,* vol. 2 (New Haven: Yale University Press, 1951); Max Winkler, *Foreign Bonds, an Autopsy* (Philadelphia: R. Swain Company,

1933); Corporation of Foreign Bondholders, *Annual Reports* (London, annually); and for a brief summary going back to 1327, Philip Wood, *The Law and Practice of International Finance* (New York: Clark Boardman Company, 1984), pp. 4.76.2 to 4.76.5.

5. See Thomas Enders and Richard Mattione, *Latin America: The Crisis of Debt and Growth* (Washington, D.C.: Brookings Institution, 1984), pp. 11-13, for a brief account of this "foreign exchange politics."

6. William Cline notes:

"It was widely recognized in the mid-1970s and again in 1979-80, that bank lending played a socially valuable role in facilitating the financial recycling of OPEC surpluses to nonoil developing countries in the process of adjustment. Official lending responded only sluggishly, especially to middle-income countries, so that it was primarily bank lending that met the sharply increased need for financing. Moreover, as was repeatedly pointed out at the time, if this lending had not been forthcoming, developing countries would have been forced to cut back their imports from industrialized countries, causing an even sharper world recession after the first oil shock."

William Cline, *International Debt and the Stability of the World Economy* (Washington, D.C.: Institute for International Economics, 1983), p. 94. For an extension of this argument, see Anatole Kaletsky, "Mad Doings in Trade," *London Review of Books,* June 21, 1984. Also Mario Henrique Simonsen, "The Developing Country Debt Problem" in Gordon Smith and John Cuddington, eds., *International Debt and the Developing Countries* (Washington, D.C.: World Bank Publications, forthcoming, 1985).

Chapter 2

1. For an unrepentant assertion of the view prevailing in the 1970s—that sovereign lending is safer than commercial banking because countries "do not go out of business," see Walter Wriston, "Banking Against Disaster," *New York Times,* September 14, 1982.

2. This so-called aleatory theory of sovereign lending (*aleator* means "dice player" in Latin) is discussed, with references, in Edwin Borchard, *State Insolvency and Foreign Bondholders: General Principles,* vol. 1 (New Haven: Yale University Press, 1951), chap. 1. Borchard's own view, which appears highly relevant to the current debt crisis, is that a default on a sovereign loan is clearly a breach of contract law but is not normally a breach of international law, which governs the relations between states. "To constitute a breach of international law [a default] must be so flagrant in character as to evidence bad faith or arbitrary discrimination justifying the bondholder's state in advancing a claim on behalf of the injured national," he says.

3. *Twycross v. Dreyfus* 5 Ch.D 605,616 (C.A. 1877).

4. E. Feilchenfeld, *Public Debts and State Succession* (1931), p. 312, quoted in M. E. Hoeflich, "Through a Glass Darkly: Reflections upon the History of the International Law of Public Debt in Connection with State Succession," *University of Illinois Law Review,* no. 1 (1982), p. 55.

5. There are, of course, two further reasons, namely, national pride and a basic sense of fairness. In periods of financial and political stability, these moral motivations are considered quite sufficient to make sovereign loans a safe investment; and even in times of crisis, lending to the governments of industrial countries is regarded as essentially risk free. However, there is an important distinction between lending to the United States or Britain and sovereign lending in general.

The U.S. government would not default on a loan because it would never need to: it could instead reduce its obligations to a manageable level through inflation. This vital point about sovereign lending is often misstated when it is asserted that the ultimate security for any government's borrowing is its unlimited ability to levy taxes. In fact, a government's taxing ability is strictly limited, both by politics and by valid supply-side economic arguments. But a government can always print new money in order to service its *own-currency* debts. Countries which are forced to borrow in foreign currencies can provide no equivalent of this guarantee through inflation.

It is worth noting in this connection that even the U.S. government has defaulted within living memory, when the guarantee through inflation was not yet acceptable to creditors. In 1933, the U.S. Congress abrogated the gold clause in all contracts, including government bonds. The Supreme Court judged this act to be a default, and one Supreme Court justice commented that "shame and humiliation is upon us; moral and financial chaos may confidently be predicted." The Congress, meanwhile, passed an act, removing suits for damages out of the Court's jurisdiction. See Borchard, p. 8; Leland Yeager, *International Monetary Relations* (New York: Harper and Row, 1966), p. 305; and Anatole Kaletsky, "Mr. Reagan Heads for Default," *Financial Times,* October 11, 1984.

6. The classic treatments are Martin Bronfenbrenner, "The Appeal of Confiscation in Economic Development," in *Economic Development and Cultural Change,* vol. 3 (1955), and Jonathan Eaton and Mark Gersowitz, "Debt with Potential Repudiation," in *Review of Economic Studies,* vol. 48 (1981).

7. For a more detailed account see William Cline, *International Debt and the Stability of the World Economy* (Washington, D.C.: Institute for International Economics, 1983), pp. 87-89, and William Cline, *International Debt: Systematic Risk and Policy Response* (Washington, D.C.: Institute for International Economics, 1984), chap. 4.

8. See Cline, *International Debt and the Stability of the World Economy,* pp. 74-82.

9. A comprehensive collection of modern theoretical analyses of the default bargain is provided in Gordon Smith and John Cuddington, eds., *International Debt and the Developing Countries,* papers presented to a symposium at the World Bank (Washington, D.C.: World Bank Publications, forthcoming, 1985).

10. Paul Krugman, "International Debt Strategies in an Uncertain World" (M.I.T., mimeograph, p. 30) and Smith and Cuddington, *International Debt and the Developing Countries.*

11. Thomas Enders and Richard Mattione, *Latin America: The Crisis of Debt and Growth* (Washington, D.C.: Brookings Institution, 1984).

12. *Ibid.,* pp. 33-50.

13. Cline, *International Debt and the Stability of the World Economy,* p. 93.

14. Few serious observers of the current financial situation would suggest that any such upsurge in lending is plausible. Although bankers frequently suggest that a resumption of "voluntary" lending to Mexico is possible in 1985 and beyond, few believe that the sums involved will be remotely comparable to the country's $10 billion to $15 billion annual interest payments—Table 2.2, for example, shows that Mexico is not expected to borrow more than $3 billion to $6 billion a year until the end of the decade.

15. Cline, *International Debt and the Stability of the World Economy,* p. 89.

16. *Ibid.,* p. 90.

Chapter 3

1. Mexico is listed with the non-oil-exporting countries under the IMF classification. Of the major borrowers, Algeria, Indonesia, Nigeria, and Venezuela are included among the oil exporters.

2. The twenty-five "major borrowers" are Algeria, Argentina, Brazil, Chile, Colombia, Egypt, Hungary, India, Indonesia, Israel, Korea, Malaysia, Mexico, Morocco, Nigeria, Pakistan, Peru, the Philippines, Portugal, Rumania, South Africa, Thailand, Turkey, Venezuela, Yugoslavia.

3. The 2.6 percent growth rate for 1985 is implied by the forecast for total commercial debts to non-oil-developing countries in Table 35 of the IMF *World Economic Outlook, Revised Projections,* September 1984.

4. If bank exposure grew by 7 percent while interest rates fell to 9 percent, new lending would be covering nearly 80 percent of the debt-

ors' interest payments. In terms of the analysis in Chapter 2, the situation would remain somewhat precarious, since interest payments would still exceed new borrowing, but it would almost certainly be manageable. The "vulnerability ratio" of 2.3 shown in Table 2.1 for 1985 would fall to 1.3.

5. The IMF itself makes the point that current problem borrowers would receive a smaller than average share of the new financing in its scenarios, while countries which have not been forced to reschedule debts would be able to expand their borrowings more rapidly than the 7 percent average rate. But this qualitative distinction understates the seriousness of the obstacles which countries like Brazil and Argentina would probably face if they sought big increases in private lending. In fact, it is one of the ironies of the current adjustment programs that countries, such as Brazil and Mexico, which have rapidly reduced their demand for external financing may find greater difficulties in returning to the capital markets than those who are still on the casualty list, like Chile and the Philippines (see Table 3.6). Morgan Guaranty Trust has done simulations from 1985 to 1990 for the Brazilian, Chilean, and Mexican economies, which assume as their "base case" a lending growth rate of zero for Brazil, 3.4 percent for Mexico, and 5.6 percent for Chile. See IMF, *World Economic Outlook*, April 1984, p. 68 and Morgan Guaranty Trust, *World Financial Markets*, October/November 1984, Table 10.

6. IMF, *World Economic Outlook*, April 1984, p. 73.

7. *Ibid.*, p. 67.

8. The figures in the tables are averages of the most recent forecasts produced by Data Resources, Inc. (DRI) and Wharton Econometrics, the two largest econometric forecasting firms in the world. For 1984 and 1985, the DRI and Wharton results have also been averaged with forecasts produced by Morgan Guaranty Trust. All these figures were based on information available through the fall of 1984.

9. Some forecasters have predicted substantially stronger trend growth for Brazil than either DRI or Wharton. Morgan Guaranty Trust has published simulations based on a 5 percent GDP growth trend from 1985 onward, which translates into 3 percent per capita growth. The projections in Cline's 1984 study assume 3 percent GDP growth in 1985 and 6 percent thereafter (that is, 1 percent and 4 percent per capita). In Cline's work, however, the growth trends are not forecasts, based on sectoral demand models, like those of DRI and Wharton; rather, they are assumptions designed to illustrate the impact which rapid growth might have on Brazil's debt situation.

Both Cline and Morgan Guaranty conclude that a GDP growth rate of 5 to 6 percent from 1985 or 1986 onward would be compatible with continuing improvements in Brazil's balance of payments. They suggest, in effect, that debt is no longer a binding constraint on Brazil's growth performance. This does not necessarily imply, however, that rapid growth rates will actually be achieved on the basis of current policies, even if the relationship between growth and the balance of payments postulated in these projections is correct. Cline argues that "domestic inflation, not the debt problem [is now] the central constraint on near-term growth"; but as he himself acknowledges, Brazil's inflation problem is closely related to its devaluations and other measures required to cope with the debt crisis.

Nevertheless, the work of Cline and Morgan Guaranty suggests that Brazil and other Latin-American countries may ultimately succeed in growing rapidly, despite their debt problems, and this indeed is the basis for the current optimism in world financial markets. However, it is premature to conclude on the basis of such projections that "the past two years have demonstrated the essential correctness of the strategy that has been followed" (Morgan Guaranty, p. 9). Such an assertion will only be possible *after* Brazil and other countries climb back onto the healthy growth paths projected by Morgan Guaranty and Cline. In the meantime, it seems prudent to take seriously the possible consequences of the DRI and Wharton forecasts proving to be more accurate than those of Morgan Guaranty and Cline. See Cline, *International Debt: Systematic Risk and Policy Response* (Washington, D.C.: Institute for International Economics, 1984), pp. 162 and 181; Morgan Guaranty Trust, *World Financial Markets*, October/November 1984.

10. Brazil's income distribution is the most unequal of any country for which such statistics are presented in the World Bank's *Development Report*. The top 10 percent of Brazil's households received 51 percent of household income, while the bottom 40 percent received only 7 percent. Corresponding figures for Mexico were 41 percent and 10 percent and for Korea 27 percent and 17 percent. *World Development Report 1984* (New York: Oxford University Press, 1984), p. 273.

11. For further details, see Thomas Enders and Richard Mattione, *Latin America: The Crisis of Debt and Growth* (Washington, D.C.: Brookings Institution, 1984), pp. 47-50.

12. All the forecasts were done on the DRI model in the spring of 1983. The figures presented in Table 3.5 would obviously be altered if the exercise were repeated on the basis of more recent policy developments and information. DRI's fall 1984 forecasts would show the following growth rates for the base case (no repudiation) presented in the first column of Table 3.5: Argentina 1.6 instead of 3.8; Brazil 1.4 instead of -1.0; Chile 2.5 instead of 4.4; Mexico 1.7 instead of 1.3; Peru -0.1 instead of 2.8; Venezuela 0.9 instead of 2.3. Data Resources Inc., *Latin American Review*, October 1984.

13. This interpretation of the Enders and Mattione simulations is at variance with the main thrust of their paper, which argues that "on economic grounds repudiation is not a better alternative for Latin America than staying with the reschedulings." However, this conclusion rests in part on the fallacy of composition—the odd notion (which is also implicit in the IMF's analysis discussed above) that no debtor country will default unless it can be shown that default would be a rational action for *every* debtor. Enders and Mattione appear to recognize this flaw in the general case against default when they state that, on political grounds, "default might be considered a real possibility at some point in the crisis for some countries, despite the absence of economic benefits from such a choice." Enders and Mattione, *Latin America: The Crisis of Debt and Growth,* p.50.

14. See Chapter 5 for a further discussion of this issue, which concludes that a conciliatory defaulter might well retain substantial short-term financing. Table 5.1 compares the gains from default with short-term credits outstanding.

Chapter 4

1. *De Haber v. Queen of Portugal* (1851) 17 Q.B. 171, 207.

2. See Bruce Nichols, "The Impact of the Foreign Sovereign Immunities Act on the Enforcement of Lenders' Remedies," *University of Illinois Law Review,* no. 1 (1982), p. 252.

3. These acts have been followed by broadly similar statutes in four other nations: Singapore (1979), Pakistan (1981), South Africa (1981), and Canada (1982). A number of continental European countries had already restricted the absolute doctrine of sovereign immunity through case law well before the British and U.S. legislation. For further details, see Philip Wood, *The Law and Practice of International Finance* (London: Sweet and Maxwell, 1982, and New York: Clark Boardman Company, 1984); "Symposium on Default by Foreign Government Debtors," *University of Illinois Law Review* 1982; Gamal Badr, *State Immunity, an Analytic and Prognostic View* (The Hague: Martinus Nijhoff, 1984). Much of the discussion in this chapter is based on these sources.

4. *Underhill and Hernandez,* 65 F. 577, 579 (2d Cir. 1895).

5. A number of Latin-American countries, including Venezuela, Colombia, and Brazil, have provisions in their constitutions which make it impossible for them to submit to the judgment of foreign courts. According to Philip Wood, "Colombian law permits no submissions to foreign laws." Venezuelan law provides that all disputes with foreign parties are to be settled in Venezuelan courts "to the exclusion of foreign claims, except where deemed inappropriate due to the nature of the con-

tract." The Brazilian government "has consistently refused to submit to the jurisdiction of foreign courts on the grounds that [it] is constitutionally incapable of doing so." However, the Brazilian government has usually accepted an arbitration clause which many lawyers regard as an implicit waiver of sovereign immunity. See Wood, *The Law and Practice of International Finance* (1984), pp. 4.8 and 4.9.

6. It is worth noting that, although the legal standing of sovereign creditors has been greatly improved in theory since 1976, many bankers are hardly even aware of this, since they have never taken very seriously the possibility of legal enforcement of sovereign loan contracts. Few would argue that the acceleration in sovereign lending in the late 1970s had anything to do with the narrowing of the legal immunity which foreign governments had previously enjoyed.

7. For a good elementary summary, see Donald Wilson, *International Business Transactions* (St. Paul, Minn: West Publishing Company, 1984), chap. 14. Also Wood, *The Law and Practice of International Finance* (1984), Section 4.11 [6].

8. *Allied Bank v. Banco Credito Agricola de Cartago,* 83-7714 (2d Cir. April 23, 1984).

9. *Banco Nacional de Cuba v. Sabbatino,* 376 U.S. 398, 421, 423 (1964).

10. *IAM v. OPEC,* 649 F.2d 1354, 1358 (9th Cir. 1981).

11. The Justice Department filed an *amicus curiae* brief on June 11, 1984, requesting the court to rehear Allied Bank's appeal on the grounds that the court had misinterpreted the foreign policy interests of the United States and that its decision would "introduce significant uncertainties into the process of making international financial arrangements . . . discourage commercial lenders . . . [and] adversely affect the taking of adjustment measures [by debtor countries]."

12. *Allied Bank v. Banco Credito Agricola de Cartago,* 566 F. Supp. 1440 (S.D.N.Y. 1983).

13. *Allied Bank v. Banco Credito Agricola de Cartago,* 83-7714 (2d Cir. April 23, 1984).

14. In any case an Act of State defense is not available to a government borrowing in its own right, since the state cannot claim to be debarred from fulfilling its obligations by its own sovereign action. See Wood, *The Law and Practice of International Finance* (1984), Section 4.11 [6], which also describes the application of the Act of State doctrine by the English and other legal systems.

15. Nichols, "The Impact of the Foreign Sovereign Immunities Act," p. 257. Nichols speaks from experience; as the senior banking partner in the Wall Street law practice of Davis, Polk & Wardwell, he led Morgan Guaranty Trust's litigation against the Iranian government in 1979.

16. For a full explanation of setoff and an exhaustive list of the various types of attachments available in normal civil litigation, see *University of Illinois Law Review* (1982), pp. 89-132; 289-304.

17. In practice a waiver of immunity from judgment may well be interpreted by U.S. or English courts as a waiver of immunity from execution. See Nichols, "The Impact of the Foreign Sovereign Immunities Act," p. 257, n. 32; see also note 20 below.

18. *Ibid.*

19. 28 U.S.C. Para. 1610 (b) (1) (1976).

20. 28 U.S.C. Para. 1610 (d) (1976). The requirement for "explicitness" of a waiver appears to be taken more seriously in the case of a prejudgment attachment than for attachment generally. Nevertheless, a recent Court of Appeals decision has thrown the lower courts' insistence on "unequivocal" waivers into some doubt. In April 1982, the 2d Circuit overruled a District Court's refusal to grant a prejudgment attachment against the government-owned Banco Nacional de Costa Rica (not to be confused with the Costa Rican Central Bank). The Banco Nacional's loan agreement contained the following waiver of immunity:

> The borrower can sue and be sued in its own name and does not have any right of immunity from suit. . . . The borrower hereby irrevocably and unconditionally waives any right or immunity from legal proceedings, including suit judgement and execution, on the grounds of sovereignty. . . .

Nonetheless, by the time the Court of Appeals had ruled that this waiver was broad enough to permit prejudgment attachment, the issue had become academic; Banco Nacional had removed $800,000 which had been briefly attached by a New York State court, closed down all of its New York bank accounts, and apparently disposed of all other assets which it may have had in the United States. *Libra Bank Limited v. Banco Nacional de Costa Rica,* U.S. District Court of New York, July 11, 1983, p. 31, describes Banco Nacional's disposal of its funds. The terms of the waiver are given in Nichols, "The Impact of the Foreign Sovereign Immunities Act," p. 260.

21. See Chapter 3, pp. 18-19.

22. 28 U.S.C. Para. 1611 (b) (1) (1976), which covers the conditions under which central bank property can be attached, is analyzed in detail by Ernest Patrikis, "Foreign Central Bank Property: Immunity from Attachment in the United States," in *University of Illinois Law Review* (1982). Patrikis, who is deputy general counsel of the Federal Reserve Bank of New York, notes that "it has been suggested that the omission of a waiver for prejudgment attachments may have been inadvertent" in the drafting of the Foreign Sovereign Immunities Act. He argues strongly,

and in effect on behalf of the New York Fed, that it was the intent of Congress to grant foreign central banks an irrevocable immunity to pre-judgment attachment and provides abundant precedents and legislative history to back up this claim. This is a view shared by the president of the New York Fed and the State Department (see below).

23. See affidavit by Anthony Solomon, president of the Federal Reserve Bank of New York, filed February 14, 1984, in *Banque Compafina v. Banco de Guatemala*, U.S. District Court (S.D.N.Y., 84 civ 1061). Solomon states:

> If foreign central banks become concerned that their assets are sub-ject to seizure and attachment by private litigants, they could be expected to withdraw their dollar denominated reserves from this country. This could cause significant liquidation of U.S. govern-ment securities holdings thereby straining the ability of the U.S. Treasury to finance the public debt and destabilizing . . . the in-ternational monetary system. Accordingly, the immunities provid-ed for foreign central banks by the Foreign Sovereign Immunities Act should be broadly construed to effect their purposes.

24. There is just one lacuna in this comfort for central bankers. In several cases against the Iranian government and its agencies, where it was impossible to grant prejudgment attachments because of the absence of waivers, U.S. courts instead issued injunctions, restraining third parties who held Iranian assets from allowing them to be transferred. The prac-tical effect of such injunctions can be identical to prejudgment at-tachments, and in some cases the U.S. government argued against grant-ing them for precisely this reason. However, in the one case which was argued in greatest detail before the 1981 Algiers Agreement suspended all litigation *(Pfizer v. Islamic Republic of Iran)*, the court order which enjoined any transfer of Iranian government property specifically ex-cluded the foreign currency reserves of the Bank Markazi Iran. See Patrikis, "Foreign Central Bank Property," p. 285.

25. See "The Legal Status of the B.I.S." in *The Bank for Interna-tional Settlements and the Basle Meetings* (Basle: B.I.S., May 1980), p. 103.

26. See Wood, *The Law and Practice of International Finance* (1982), p. 101. In the most recent English case, *S.P.P. (Middle East) Limited v. Arab Republic of Egypt*, the Court of Appeal, on March 19, 1984, denied a Mareva injunction on the National Bank of Egypt's reserves at the Bank of England and a number of commercial banks. But the court did not address the question of sovereign immunity directly, stating on-ly that "the problem of whether it is proper to make such an order against

a foreign sovereign state" was an issue which would have to be resolved with "assistance from an *amicus curiae*" (presumably the Bank of England and the government).

27. Even in cases where 100 percent of a private company's stock was owned by a single individual, the company's assets have been distinguished from those of the owner. (See Wood, *The Law and Practice of International Finance* (1984), p. 4.36). In the shipping business, it is a commonplace practice to register every ship in the name of a separate "one-ship company" for the specific purpose of avoiding maritime arrest when a sister ship is embroiled in legal disputes.

28. This judgment by the British House of Lords referred to a dispute between Cuba and Chile over sugar cargos diverted by the Cuban government after it learned of the overthrow of the Allende regime. The case is known by the name of the ship involved: *I Congresso del Partido* (1981) 3 W.L.R. 2328 (H.L.). For a strong rebuttal of the "corporate veil" theory as it applies to state trading companies in Communist countries, see A. H. Hermann, *Conflicts of National Laws with International Business Activity* (London: British-North American Committee, 1982), chap. 2.

29. Wood, *The Law and Practice of International Finance* (1984), p. 4.35, referring to *Minpeco S.A. v. Conti Commodities Services Inc.*, 549 F. Supp. 857 (1982), a dispute between a Peruvian government mining company and a U.S. commodity broker.

30. Other well-known cases where damages for governmental actions have apparently been levied against the property of government-owned trading companies include the Cuban sugar cases mentioned in note 28 above, in which the Cuban ship *I Congresso del Partido* was temporarily arrested for a default by Cubazucar, the state sugar monopoly. This arrest was justified because the ship was owned by the Cuban government itself and the government was also a defendant in the action by Chilean plaintiffs. In 1973, the French courts allowed the Braden Copper Company, whose assets had been expropriated by the Chilean government, to seize certain copper shipments from Chile into France. In this case, however, the point at issue was the legal ownership of the copper being exported by Chile. According to the French court, Chile's expropriation did not confer upon its government a legal title to what had been Braden's copper. Curiously, German courts took the opposite view on identical facts. See Wood, *The Law and Practice of International Finance* (1982), p. 130.

31. The impact of these indirect costs and benefits on bankers' motivations may be one explanation for what little litigation there has been against sovereign debtors since 1981. The only lawsuits have been against small countries like Guatemala and Costa Rica. These countries could

do little damage even if they retaliated strongly against the banks after a seriously adverse judgment. The litigation has been led by small banks. Some of these may have largely written off their losses in the countries in question and could therefore indulge in nuisance suits, perhaps in the hope of being bought out of loan syndicates by bigger and more nervous banks. It is also interesting, however, that Libra Bank, one of the leaders in the litigation against Costa Rica, is actually a consortium bank owned by several major European institutions; presumably, it must have been testing the legal waters with their approval.

32. See Nichols, "The Impact of the Foreign Sovereign Immunities Act," pp. 260-63, for an argument that "the heightened awareness of legal risks (since the Iranian imbroglio) undoubtedly influences illiquid governments to seek prompt negotiations with their creditors." Despite this assertion, however, Nichols concludes that "the major factors bringing debtor countries to the bargaining table sooner than in the past have been economic and political, rather than legal."

Chapter 5

1. Quoted in Michael Sesit, "Debt Crisis Hurts Multinational Concerns, Limiting Markets and Complicating Funding," *Wall Street Journal,* June 8, 1984.

2. Cuba, one of the very few countries that has ever stated openly that it was *unwilling* to honor its debts or consider compensation for expropriated U.S. interests, had nonetheless built up some $3.2 billion in debts to non–U.S. banks and Western governments by 1983. These debts were rescheduled in March 1983 and July 1984 by the "Paris Club" of Western government creditors. Cuba's ability to borrow as much per head as Indonesia or Thailand, in a period of twenty years after a major debt repudiation and foreign asset confiscation, provides an eloquent example of the lack of solidarity among creditor nations and private banks in response to defaults. See Brian Reading, *Monthly Monitor* (New York: HME International Advisory Associates, November 1984), pp. 96–97.

3. The growing awareness among multinationals that they are "the forgotten victims in the strategic warfare going on between debtor countries and the banks," in the words of John Basek, a partner in Multinational Strategies Inc., has led a group of U.S. industrial companies to explore the possibility of establishing a new organization—the Corporate Council on International Finance—"to explore better ways of protecting the interest of multinationals in the debt–rescheduling process." See Sesit, "Debt Crisis Hurts Multinational Concerns," and Norman Bailey, *Reviving International Trade Financing* (Washington, D.C.: International Business–Government Counsellors, February 1984).

4. See Tables 2.2 and 3.6.

5. On Cuba, see note 2 above. For the historical experience, see references in Chapter 1, note 4. In 1938, 73 percent by value of all the bonds issued to Latin–American countries were in default. Although these defaults were eventually rectified, the terms were extremely unfavorable to creditors, who rarely received more than twenty or thirty cents on the dollar; see note 15 below.

6. See Anatole Kaletsky, "Seizing Assets Is Not So Easy," *Financial Times,* June 25, 1984.

7. Council of the Americas, *The`Impact of the Economic Crisis in Argentina, Brazil, Mexico and Venezuela on U.S. Companies* (New York: The Americas Society, September 1984).

8. Evidence of this has already begun to emerge in Mexico and Brazil; see, for examples, Sesit, "Debt Crisis Hurts Multinational Concerns"; James Buxton, "Fiat Automoveis Turns to Exports as It Waits on Brazilian Expectations," *Financial Times,* June 20, 1984, and Hugh O'Shaughnessy, "LA Eases Way for Investors," *The Financial Times,* December 12, 1984. However, direct investment is unlikely to make more than a modest contribution to resolving the debt crisis, even if it resumes the rapid buildup of 1975–82, when it was flowing into Latin America at a rate of over $3 billion annually. This is because a high proportion of direct investment "inflows" consist of the reinvestment of locally generated earnings by overseas subsidiaries of multinational companies. Since 1972, reinvested earnings have always provided 60 percent or more of direct investment inflows by U.S. companies. See U.S. Department of Commerce, *International Direct Investment* (Washington, D.C.: U.S. Government Printing Office, August 1984), Tables 4 and 11; and Martin Gilman, *The Financing of Foreign Direct Investment* (London: Frances Pinter Publishers, 1981).

9. For an assessment of Brazil's importance to Citicorp see Thomas Hanley, "Citibank Brazil; A Microcosm of Citicorp by 1990," *Salomon Brothers Bank Securities Department Research Newsletter* (New York: Salomon Brothers, April 1984); see also Alan Riding, "In Indebted Brazil, Citicorp Earns a Record Profit," *International Herald Tribune,* December 4, 1984.

10. Trade financing arrangements which bypass the major commercial banks have always existed, but the number and complexity of these schemes has multiplied as a result of the debt crisis. There have been cases, particularly involving Poland, in which the trade financing arms of major international banks which were refusing to lend to Poland directly were nonetheless providing trade finance through the forfait market and bonds insured, for example, at Lloyd's of London. For details, see the monthly *Euromoney Trade Finance Report* and case studies in *Case*

Histories in Trade Financing (London: Euromoney Publications, 1984).

11. In Nigeria's case, a very high proportion of the foreign debt —perhaps as much as 50 percent—was in the form of short–term obligations and private sector commercial credits, many of them unrecorded in banking statistics. This made it impossible for the country to give preference to trade creditors. For estimates of Nigeria's debts, see Amex Bank Review Special Papers, *International Debts, Banks, and the LDCs* (London: American Express International Banking Corporation, March 1984).

12. See the questionnaire study cited in note 7 above for information on multinationals' internal trade financing policies.

13. In principle, most official export credit institutions are run on strict insurance principles, with the cost of cover reflecting the loss experience for that type of cover and the country in question. Obviously, political considerations will sometimes override purely commercial calculations. This can work both ways, as in the case of Poland, which is expected to regain its access to Western governments' trade finance facilities more as a result of the lifting of martial law and an amnesty for political prisoners, despite the worst record of defaulting on intergovernment debts in recent history. See Reading, *Monthly Monitor,* pp. 81–84.

14. From a legal standpoint, the preferential servicing of trade debts over medium–term debts is an established feature of sovereign lending arrangements. Even in the very tightly worded rescheduling agreements of recent years, which stipulate that no other debts can be repaid on more favorable terms than the debts rescheduled, specific exemption is normally made for trade debts. The rationale is the universal recognition that a country needs to trade in order to have any chance of remaining solvent. See Philip Wood, *The Law and Practice of International Finance* (New York: Clark Boardman Company, 1984), pp. 4.130, 4.142.

15. For examples, see sources cited in note 10 above.

Chapter 6

1. According to the *New York Times* of May 8, 1943, President Roosevelt took the occasion of a state visit by General Penarada, president of Bolivia, to offer an apology for "some Americans [who] sold to the Bolivian government through supersalesmanship the idea that it needed a loan." After deducting the bankers' commissions, Bolivia received only 92 percent of the proceeds. "Of course, the President declared, Bolivia was unable to pay either the interest or the principal," the *Times* reported. This incident is cited in Edwin Borchard, *State Insolvency and Foreign Bondholders,* vol. 1 (New Haven: Yale University Press, 1951), p. 243. For other references see Chapter 1, note 4.

2. "Recognizing that we could not police every country south of the Rio Grande and that forceful measures in one country raised up new enemies in other parts of the Hemisphere, our policy shifted to non-intervention and good neighborliness." This characterization of U.S. policy on defaults in the 1930s remains valid today. See Willy Feuerlein and Elizabeth Hannan, *Dollars in Latin America* (New York: Council on Foreign Relations, 1941), pp. 30–39 and 80–81.

3. Cuba and Iran are the most obvious examples.

4. See William Clark, *Catastrophe* (London: Sidgwick & Jackson, 1984), for a fictional but well-informed account of how retaliation against a Third World debtors' cartel could lead to worldwide economic warfare and ultimately a collapse of economic and political institutions in the developing countries. Clark was at one time a vice-president of the World Bank.

5. See Table 3.5 for the orders of magnitude involved.

6. For further details, see David Wyss and Ron Napier, "The World Debt Crisis and the U.S. Economy," *Data Resources U.S. Review* (Lexington, Mass.: D.R.I., September 1983) and *What If Latin America Defaults?* (Philadelphia: Wharton Econometric Forecasting Associates, fall 1984). These analyses differ considerably in various assumptions, but both postulate what the present study calls a "conciliatory" default, that is, the debtor countries announce a temporary suspension of interest payments and are not subjected to economic sanctions. However, both these studies assume, without explanation, a sharp fall in U.S. exports to Latin America. In the Wharton simulation, Latin America's imports plunge by $17 billion, despite the availability of $20 billion of additional foreign exchange to the defaulting countries after the suspension of interest payments. It is this fall in imports which accounts for the catastrophic 9 percent decline in Latin America's GNP that Wharton projects. The analysis in Chapter 5 suggests that the assumption of a collapse in imports is unrealistic.

7. *Ibid.*

8. For a fuller explanation of how bank illiquidity and multiple credit contraction would be related, see William Cline, *International Debt and the Stability of the World Economy* (Washington, D.C.: Institute for International Finance, 1983), pp. 36–40; Mark Fulton, "The U.S. Banking System and Latin America," *James Capel Economic Service Newsletter* (London: James Capel & Co., June 1984); and Samuel Brittan, "If the Banks Need Help," *Financial Times,* June 28, 1984.

9. See "Fed Pledges It Will Lend 'Boldly,'" *Financial Times,* May 29, 1984.

10. "U.S. Won't Let Biggest Banks in Nation Fail," *Wall Street Journal,* September 20, 1984.

11. See Brittan, "If the Banks Need Help."

12. From the first quarter of 1982 to the fourth quarter of 1983, stock prices for money center banks fell by 30 percent relative to the Standard and Poor 500 Index; regional bank stocks declined only 4 percent. See George Salem, "Fourth-Quarter Review and 1984 Outlook," *Becker Paribas Banking Industry Service* (New York: A. G. Becker Paribas Inc., February 1984). For more evidence on shareholder skepticism about international banking, see Thomas Hanley, "Bank Stocks, The Ongoing Quest for Purity," *Salomon Brothers Bank Securities Department Research Newsletter* (New York: Salomon Brothers, April 1984) and Daniel Hertzberg, "U.S. Banks Face Investor Wariness Due to Strategy on Foreign Loans," *Wall Street Journal* (Europe), June 13, 1984.

13. Furthermore, the relative importance of the biggest banks in the U.S. economy has been declining. At the end of 1980, the ten biggest banks held 17.9 percent of the banking system's total deposits, against 20.2 percent in 1970. See "Developments in Banking Structure 1970–81," *Federal Reserve Bulletin,* February 1982, pp. 77–85.

This breakdown of the banks' exposure by size is not supposed to imply that the collapse of the largest banks in the country would be an acceptable consequence of default to the U.S. government or the economy. It does underline, however, the fact that the banks are by no means "all in the same boat" on this issue. This becomes particularly significant because of the current deregulation in the banking industry. Deregulation is seen as a mortal threat by many small regional banks. Many of them are therefore relieved, rather than distressed, by the way the sovereign debt crisis has weakened the capital positions and stock market ratings of the money center banks. These small banks, which constitute a powerful political lobby, are unlikely to welcome any government action which gets the big banks off the sovereign debt hook unless such action also requires the big banks to strengthen their capital ratios and hence slow their pace of expansion.

14. "Panel Questions FDIC Warnings in Bank Bailout," *Wall Street Journal,* October 5, 1984.

15. In the great majority of past defaults, some payments have eventually been made to creditors, albeit on a much reduced scale and after many years. For example, Mexico's loans, which had mostly been in default since the mid-1920s, started being redeemed in 1946, but only at around 20 percent of face value, and interest arrears were settled at less than one cent on the dollar. See Anatole Kaletsky, "When the Debtors Said No," *Financial Times,* December 28, 1983, and Corporation of Foreign Bondholders, *Annual Report 1967,* pp. 202–15, for a history of the Mexican, Brazilian, and other Latin-American debts. However, all the Latin-American governments which defaulted in the 1930s and

settled their debts in the 1940s and 1950s had from the start averred their *willingness* to pay; in theory they were merely awaiting an improvement in economic conditions: they were conciliatory defaulters. Of the governments which have formally repudiated their debts this century—including the USSR, China, Cuba, and North Korea—only the USSR has bothered to reach even a symbolic settlement with creditors. *Wall Street Journal*, July 10, 1984.

16. The fact that subjective judgments must be made both about the size of the ultimate loss and about the precise point in time when the bank can be said to have lost the money is one of the redeeming features of a conciliatory default that has made the debt crisis manageable so far, even when countries like Argentina have built up lengthy arrears. Even loans to Poland, Zaire, and Bolivia, which have not made any interest or principal payments for several years, still stand in the books of the banks at a sizable proportion of their full values. If these countries had declared their unwillingness to pay, such treatment would have been much harder to justify. For an excellent description of the inevitable subjectivity in bank accounting for sovereign loans, see Colin Brown, "LDC Debts—the Accounting and Auditing Response," *Institute of Chartered Accountants Banking Conference 1984* (London: Institute of Chartered Accountants, May 1984).

17. This figure assumes an average interest rate of 12 percent on loans which total about twelve times the money center banks' pretax earnings.

18. See "Fed Proposes Cap on Interest Rates for International Loans," *Financial Times*, May 4, 1984, and a letter from Emminger, "Dealing with the Debt Crisis," *Financial Times*, May 8, 1984.

19. See Table 6.3.

20. See Anatole Kaletsky, "A Way Round the Debt Crisis," *Financial Times*, August 9, 1984, and Hertzberg, "U.S. Banks Face Investor Wariness."

21. For example, forgiving 5 percent of the interest and establishing loss reserves equal to 4 percent of the exposure each year would require a total of 9 percentage points in interest payments to be deducted from profits. This would reduce the big banks' profits by 81 percent according to Table 6.4; Bank of America, Chase Manhattan, Manufacturers Hanover, and, of course, Continental Illinois, would all be forced into loss. With minute or nonexistent profits, it would be impossible for these banks to keep their capital bases growing in line with inflation, and there would be a serious danger that their exposure to problem debtors, relative to capital, would increase, rather than decrease, even despite the rapid rate of loss reserving.

Chapter 7

1. See Chapter 5.

2. In 1982, 87 percent of U.S. imports from Latin America were categorized as food and animals, crude materials, and mineral fuels; 74 percent of U.S. exports to Latin America were chemicals, machinery, transport equipment, and other manufactured goods. Between 1978 and 1981 (that is, in the last four years before the debt crisis), the United States enjoyed a surplus of $2.04 billion in its merchandise trade with Latin America; excluding U.S. imports of oil, this surplus was roughly $50 billion over the four-year period. See also "U.S. Trade with Latin America: Consequences of Finance Constraints," *Federal Reserve Bank of New York Quarterly Review,* Autumn 1983.

3. See Norman Bailey, "The Response of the Government of the United States to the International Debt Crisis," *Report to SELA Conference Caracas* (Washington, D.C.: International Business-Government Counsellors, May 1984).

4. Thomas Enders and Richard Mattione, *Latin America: The Crisis of Debt and Growth* (Washington, D.C.: Brookings Institution, 1984), p. 56 (emphasis added). See also the speeches by Norman Bailey, formerly of the National Security Council, quoted at the head of this chapter and note 3 above.

5. There is an institutional rider which reinforces this point. The initiative for foreign policy retaliation in the event of a default, for example, through trade embargoes or asset seizures, would have to come from the State Department and the White House, which could be expected to show more awareness of the diplomatic consequences of U.S. actions than the Treasury or the Federal Reserve.

6. See "Confidence, Conciliation, and Cash Flow" in Chapter 6.

7. The policy on defaults adopted by the U.S. government in the 1930s seems relevant and instructive:

> Formally the United States government requires that other states shall respect their obligations vis-a-vis American creditors, and that in case payments are scaled down or delayed American creditors shall receive treatment as good as that accorded foreign creditors. Our government will protect against repudiation by a foreign government . . . it will protest discrimination against (American citizens). But it will *not* undertake to determine how fully, at what date, and in what currency the obligations of a debtor country shall be fulfilled. The fact that a foreign government acknowledges responsibility for payment and promises equal treatment (irrespective of how good or how bad) satisfies, in form at least, the United States government.

Willy Feuerlein and Elizabeth Hannan, *Dollars in Latin America* (New York: Council on Foreign Relations, 1941), p. 30.

8. See Chapter 1, note 1 for a comparison between Brazil's and Japan's trade performances.

9. What will happen to the IMF's relationship with countries like Mexico and Brazil once the current three-year standby programs expire in 1986 is still unclear. In the long-term rescheduling agreed between Mexico and the banks, there is a presumption that Mexico will continue regular consultations with the IMF but will not be subject to any formal targets. This has been taken to imply that Mexico will free itself from effective IMF surveillance by 1986. It is often forgotten, however, that Mexico's long-term rescheduling does not involve any new money from the banks. When Mexico and Brazil are forced to return to the private capital markets for substantial amounts of money, it remains to be seen whether this will be made available without IMF policy strings.

10. The ideological conservatives who campaigned in 1983 against the IMF Bill in Congress were, of course, extremely vocal in putting forward this little argument.

11. See note 4 above.

12. See, for example, the comments on the Chilean and Argentine economic experiments, "which enjoyed a good reputation in IMF circles," by Mario Henrique Simonsen in the World Bank symposium cited in Chapter 2, note 9.

13. IMF, *World Economic Outlook,* April 1984, p. 76.

14. *Ibid.,* p. 25.

Chapter 8

1. "Regan Calls for Government to Limit Debt Role," *Financial Times,* May 30, 1984.

2. The unexpected replacement of William Dale, the IMF's deputy managing director, by Richard Erb, formerly the U.S. executive director on the IMF Board, in the summer of 1984 was widely viewed as a reflection of U.S. dominance over the Fund's policies.

3. This process has already begun to some extent, with the amended regulations for international banks adopted in February 1984 by the Federal Reserve Board and the comptroller of the currency to implement the International Lending Supervisions Act, and with subsequent directions by U.S. regulators to individual banks.

4. See Colin Brown, "LDC Debts—the Accounting and Auditing Response," *Institute of Chartered Accountants Banking Conference* (London: Institute of Chartered Accountants, 1984).

5. See Chapter 6, note 18. The *Amex Bank Review,* vol. 11, no. 5 (London: American Express International Banking Corporation, June 1984), contains a useful summary of some of the main restructuring proposals.

6. Nicholas Colchester, "Interest Relief from the IMF," *Financial Times,* May 3, 1984; "Brazil Set to Propose Interest Safety Net for Debtor States," *Financial Times,* May 18, 1984.

7. See John Williamson, *A New SDR Allocation?* (Washington, D.C.: Institute for International Economics, March 1984).

8. See Table 6.6.

9. Assuming that loan loss reserves were created at the rate of 4 percent of outstanding exposures and a further 2 percent of interest was forgiven, the reduction in earnings for money center banks would average 54 percent; they would vary from 35 percent for Morgan to 79 percent for Manufacturers Hanover. If shareholders' equity grew by 5 percent a year, the banks' average exposure to the six major problem borrowers would fall to 121 percent by 1994 and 82 percent by 2004. If shareholders' equity grew by 10 percent a year, exposure would fall to 76 percent by 1994 and 32 percent by 2004. See Tables 6.5 and 6.6.

10. For Latin America as a whole, the ratio of debt to GNP in 1984 is estimated as 45.6 percent by the IMF. With debt growing at 2 percent and GNP growing at 5 percent, this ratio would decline to 34.3 percent by 1994 and 25.6 percent in 2004. IMF, *World Economic Outlook Revised Projections,* September 1984, p. 69.

11. The publicly guaranteed debt of all developing countries to financial institutions in 1984 was $289 billion, according to the IMF; 2 percent of this would be $5.8 billion. If all government guaranteed debts to private creditors were included in the restructuring, creditor country governments would have to lend the Third World an additional $6.8 billion annually. Assuming the World Bank retained the capital structure agreed at the last General Capital Increase, in 1980, governments would have to pay in 7.5 percent of the increase in capital; thus to raise $6.8 billion of new capital for the World Bank annually, governments would have to pay in $510 million a year. For an explanation of the World Bank's capital structure, see *World Bank Annual Report 1984,* p. 76.

Tables

Table 1.1
Debt and Trade Aggregates for Developing Countries ($ bn)

	1978	1979	1980	1981	1982	1983	1984	1985
All developing countries								
Debt	**396**	**469**	**559**	**651**	**741**	**782**	**827**	**863**
Exports (f.o.b.)	342	466	617	612	536	507	558	607
Imports (f.o.b.)	333	408	523	572	528	489	516	560
Trade Balance	9	58	94	40	8	18	42	47
Non-oil developing countries								
Debt	**343**	**404**	**485**	**572**	**650**	**686**	**729**	**645**
Exports (f.o.b.)	198	254	321	338	322	332	374	413
Imports (f.o.b.)	235	307	397	422	376	356	385	422
Trade balance	-37	-53	-76	-84	-53	-24	-11	-9
Seven largest borrowers[1]								
Debt	**156**	**191**	**234**	**286**	**338**	**350**	**370**	**385**
Exports (f.o.b.)	62	82	109	123	112	113	129	143
Imports (f.o.b.)	64	81	104	116	101	82	92	101
Trade balance	-2	1	5	7	11	31	37	42
Western Hemisphere								
Debt	**133**	**158**	**193**	**247**	**288**	**299**	**315**	**328**
Exports (f.o.b.)	45	58	75	80	75	76	85	95
Imports (f.o.b.)	47	63	85	91	71	55	60	66
Trade balance	-2	-5	-10	-11	3	21	25	28

[1]Argentina, Brazil, Indonesia, Korea, Mexico, Philippines, and Venezuela.
Source: IMF *World Economic Outlook*, Revised Projections, September 1984.

Table 1.2
Trade and Interest Payments ($ bn)
(Total external debt of each country in 1984 in brackets)

	1981	1984	1989
Argentina ($45 bn)			
Exports (goods)	9.1	8.4	12.5
Imports (goods)	9.4	4.3	7.9
Trade balance (goods)	-0.3	4.1	4.6
Service balance (excluding interest)	-0.8	0.1	1.6
Interest payments	3.5	5.7	7.4
Brazil ($98 bn)			
Exports (goods)	23.3	26.4	42.5
Imports (goods)	22.1	14.3	28.5
Trade balance (goods)	1.2	12.1	14.0
Service balance (excluding interest)	-3.3	-2.6	-2.4
Interest payments	9.8	11.2	14.1
Chile ($20 bn)			
Exports (goods)	4.0	3.9	6.6
Imports (goods)	6.6	3.3	5.4
Trade balance (goods)	-2.6	0.6	1.2
Service balance (excluding interest)	-0.2	-0.3	0.2
Interest payments	1.9	2.3	3.5
Mexico ($88 bn)			
Exports (goods)	19.4	23.0	39.6
Imports (goods)	25.1	11.0	29.5
Trade balance (goods)	-5.7	12.0	10.1
Service balance (excluding interest)	-1.7	0.0	-5.1
Interest payments	8.4	10.9	13.2
Venezuela ($34 bn)			
Exports (goods)	19.5	15.0	23.6
Imports (goods)	12.1	8.5	14.1
Trade balance (goods)	7.4	6.5	9.5
Service balance (excluding interest)	0.5	-0.3	1.5
Interest payments	3.9	4.3	4.7

Table 1.2 (continued)

	1981	1984	1989
Korea ($42 bn)			
Exports (goods)	20.7	27.5	54.3
Imports (goods)	24.3	28.9	56.8
Trade balance (goods)	-3.6	-1.4	-2.5
Service balance (excluding interest)	1.1	0.8	1.5
Interest payments	3.0	3.8	4.9
Philippines ($26 bn)			
Exports (goods)	5.7	4.5	6.2
Imports (goods)	7.9	5.9	8.2
Trade balance (goods)	-2.2	-1.4	-2.0
Service balance (excluding interest)	0.2	0.3	0.5
Interest Payments	1.1	1.9	2.5

Source: Wharton Econometric Forecasting Associates, *World Economic Outlook*, October 1984.

Table 2.1
Interest Payments, New Borrowing, and "Vulnerability Ratios"[1]

	1978	1979	1980	1981	1982	1983	1984	1985
All developing countries								
Interest payments (A)[2]	22	32	46	61	71	65	72	81
New borrowing (B)[2]	68	73	90	92	90	41	45	36
Ratio[1] (A÷B)	0.3	0.4	0.5	0.7	0.8	1.6	1.6	2.3
Western hemisphere								
Interest payments (A)[2]	9	14	20	29	36	33	35	37
New borrowing (B)[2]	23	25	35	54	41	11	16	13
Ratio[1] (A÷B)	0.4	0.6	0.6	0.5	0.9	3.0	2.2	2.8

[1]A ratio of more than one means that interest payments exceed net new borrowing. This indicates a vulnerability to default (see text).

[2]Interest payments and new borrowing are expressed in billions of dollars.

Source: Author's calculations based on IMF *World Outlook*, Revised Projections, September 1984.

Table 2.2
"Vulnerability Ratios"[1] through 1989 for Latin-American Debtors

	1981	1982	1983	1984	1985	1986	1987	1988	1989
Argentina									
Interest (A)[2]	4	5	5	6	7	7	6	6	7
New borrowing (B)[2]	6	4	7	2	2	2	1	1	0
Ratio[1] (A÷B)	0.7	1.3	0.7	3.0	3.5	3.5	6.0	6.0	*
Brazil									
Interest (A)	10	11	10	11	14	14	12	13	14
New borrowing (B)	7	10	9	4	1	3	4	2	1
Ratio[1] (A÷B)	1.4	1.1	1.1	2.7	14.0	4.7	3.0	6.5	14.0
Chile									
Interest (A)	2	3	2	2	3	3	3	3	4
New borrowing (B)	5	2	1	1	2	2	2	2	1
Ratio[1] (A÷B)	0.4	1.5	2.0	2.0	1.5	1.5	1.5	1.5	4.0
Mexico									
Interest (A)	8	11	10	11	14	13	11	12	13
New borrowing (B)	23	9	3	2	3	3	3	5	6
Ratio[1] (A÷B)	0.3	1.2	3.3	5.5	4.7	4.3	3.7	2.4	2.2
Venezuela									
Interest (A)	4	3	4	4	5	5	4	4	5
New borrowing (B)	1	4	2	1	0	2	1	0	0
Ratio[1] (A÷B)	4.0	0.8	2.0	4.0	*	2.5	4.0	*	*

[1]A ratio of more than one means that interest payments exceed net new borrowing. This indicates a vulnerability to default (see text).   [2]Interest and new borrowing are expressed in billions of dollars.   *The ratio of interest to new borrowing in these years is theoretically infinite.

Source: Author's calculations based on forecasts in Wharton Econometric Forecasting Associates, *Latin American Economic Outlook*, October 1984, and Data Resources Inc., *Latin American Review*, Fall 1984.

Table 3.1
IMF Forecasts
Annual percentage changes in real GDP

	Average 1967-76	1980	1981	1982	1983	1984	1985	Average 1985-90
Non-oil developing countries	5.6	5.0	3.1	1.7	1.8	3.7	4.3	4.6[1]
Seven largest borrowers	6.5	4.7	1.8	0.4	-1.1	1.8	4.0	4.4[1]
Western hemisphere	6.6	6.0	1.1	-1.2	-2.8	1.1	3.4	*

[1]"Base scenario" in medium-term projections—this figure refers to the twenty-five largest borrowers, not just the seven included in the other forecasts.

*Medium-term projections do not give geographical breakdown. Forecasts by Wharton Econometrics and Data Resources project an average growth rate of 3.1 per-cent for the 1985-90 period.

Source: IMF *World Economic Outlook*, Revised Projections, September 1984.

Table 3.2
IMF Medium-term Projections for Non-oil LDCs
(percentage changes and interest rates)

	1985	1986	1987	1988	1989-1990
Base scenario					
OECD growth	3.2	3.2	3.2	3.2	3.2
Interest rates[1]	12.0	10.0	10.0	9.0	9.0
Private lending growth[2]	(3)[3]	7.0	7.0	7.0	7.0
LDC export growth	5.4	5.4	5.4	5.3	5.3
LDC import growth	6.2	6.2	6.2	6.1	6.1
LDC growth	4.6	4.6	4.6	4.6	4.6
Pessimistic scenario[4]					
OECD growth	2.2	2.2	2.2	2.2	2.2
Interest rates[1]	13.0	11.0	11.0	10.0	10.0
LDC growth	4.6	3.5	3.5	3.5	3.5
Crisis scenario[4]					
OECD growth	3.2	2.2	1.2	2.2	3.2
Private lending growth[2]	(3)[3]	6.0	3.0	6.0	7.0
LDC growth	4.6	3.5	3.5	3.5	3.5
Weak policy scenario[4]					
LDC export growth	5.4	4.4	4.4	4.3	4.3
LDC import growth	6.2	7.2	7.2	7.1	7.1
LDC growth	4.6	4.8	4.8	4.8	4.8

[1]Average interest rate on developing countries' commercial debt. The IMF assumes the 1985 level will be equal to that of 1984 and that the rate will then decline in 1986 and 1988. The figures shown are based on an average 12 percent rate actually paid by Brazil in 1984.

[2]Growth of total commercial lending to LDCs, including export credits.

[3]Actual growth rate forecast in IMF *World Economic Outlook*, Revised Projections, September 1984.

[4]All parameters except for the ones indicated are identical to Base Scenario.

Source: Author's inferences from IMF *World Economic Outlook*, April 1984.

Table 3.3
Consensus Growth Forecasts for Major Debtors[1]
(annual percentage changes given)

	1960–1970	1970–1981	1981	1982	1983	1984	1985	1986	1987	1988	1989
Argentina	4.3	1.9	-6.2	-5.3	2.8	3.2	-0.3	1.8	3.1	2.4	3.4
Brazil	5.4	8.4	-1.9	1.4	-3.3	1.8	3.6	3.0	3.8	4.2	4.3
Chile	4.4	2.1	5.7	-14.3	-0.9	5.3	2.2	3.3	1.8	3.2	5.3
Colombia	5.1	5.7	2.5	0.9	0.8	1.7	1.5	2.6	3.2	3.6	3.9
Mexico	7.6	6.5	7.9	-0.5	-4.7	1.5	4.0	4.3	5.1	5.8	5.3
Peru	4.9	3.0	3.1	0.7	-11.0	1.5	3.7	2.1	1.8	2.0	3.6
Venezuela	6.0	4.5	0.4	0.7	-4.8	-0.4	2.5	3.0	3.5	3.1	3.5
Indonesia	3.9	7.8	7.6	2.2	4.0	4.5	5.0	4.4	5.5	5.0	5.3
Korea	8.6	9.1	7.1	5.5	9.3	7.9	7.0	5.8	6.5	6.8	6.5
Malaysia	6.5	7.8	6.7	5.2	5.6	6.6	5.8	5.4	6.4	6.3	6.3
Philippines	5.1	6.2	3.8	3.0	1.0	-4.8	0.3	2.7	3.5	4.0	4.1
Thailand	8.4	7.2	6.3	4.2	5.8	5.3	5.9	5.1	6.4	6.2	6.3

[1]These figures are obtained by averaging forecasts made by Data Resources Inc., Wharton Econometric Forecasting Associates, and (for 1984 and 1985 only) Morgan Guaranty Trust.

Sources: Wharton Econometric Forecasting Associates, World Economic Outlook, October 1984; Data Resources Inc., Latin American Review, Fall 1984; Data Resources, Inc., Asian Review, Summer 1984; Morgan Guaranty Trust, World Financial Markets, October/November 1984.

Table 3.4
Per Capita Growth Trends
(average annual changes in real GDP per capita)

	1960-1981	1981-1983	1984	1985	1986-1989	Change in trend[1]
Argentina	1.9	-4.1	1.9	-1.6	1.4	-0.5
Brazil	5.1	-3.9	-0.2	1.6	1.8	-3.3
Chile	0.7	-4.6	3.9	0.8	1.8	+1.1
Colombia	3.2	-0.5	-0.2	-0.4	1.4	-1.8
Mexico	3.8	-1.4	-0.8	1.5	2.8	-1.0
Peru	1.0	-4.6	-1.2	2.2	0.2	-0.8
Venezuela	2.4	-3.8	-3.4	-0.3	0.7	-1.7
Indonesia	4.1	2.7	2.6	3.1	3.2	-0.9
Korea	6.9	5.9	6.5	5.6	5.3	-1.6
Malaysia	4.3	3.8	4.6	3.8	4.1	-0.2
Philippines	2.8	0.5	-6.9	-1.8	1.1	-1.7
Thailand	4.6	3.5	3.4	4.0	4.1	-0.5

[1]Difference between column 5 and column 1.

Source: Author's calculations based on Table 3.3 and World Bank, *World Development Report* (1984).

Table 3.5
Effects of Repudiation as Estimated by Enders and Mattione
(Annualized growth of GDP over five years 1983-87)

	No repudiation[5]	Repudiation with:	
		5 percent cost[1]	10 percent cost[1]
Argentina	3.8	4.6	4.4
Brazil	-1.0	2.3[2]	1.0[2]
Chile	4.4	3.4[2]	1.3[2]
Mexico	1.3	2.9[3]	-0.1[3]
Peru	2.8	1.5[4]	-1.5[4]
Venezuela	2.3	5.7[2]	5.2[3]

[1]See text for explanation.

[2]Less than two months reserves in first year.

[3]Less than one month reserves in first year.

[4]Negative reserves in first year.

[5]Forecasts made by Data Resources Inc. in spring of 1983. More recent forecasts are shown in Table 3.3 and footnote 3.11.

Source: Author's calculations based on Enders and Mattione, *Latin America: The Crisis of Debt and Growth* (Washington, D.C.: Brookings Institution, 1984), Table 13.

Table 3.6
The Temptation to Default[1]
($ bn annually from 1985 to 1989)

	Total Interest payments	New Loans expected	Crude gain from default	Interest on official credits	Interest on short-term credits	Temptation to default	Difference between 1985 imports and peak imports[2]
Argentina	6.5	1.2	5.3	0.6	1.4	3.3	(3.3)
Brazil	13.4	3.5	9.9	0.5	0.6	8.8	(7.4)
Chile	3.0	1.8	1.2	0.1	0.2	0.9	(2.9)
Mexico	13.0	4.2	8.8	0.6	0.4	7.8	(10.4)
Peru	1.6	1.3	0.3	0.2	0.1	0	(1.3)
Venezuela	4.4	0.5	3.9	0.2	0.4	3.3	(2.7)
Philippines	2.2	2.7	-0.5	0.4	1.2	-2.1	(2.0)

[1]These figures are based on averages of forecasts made by Data Resources Inc. and Wharton Econometric Forecasting Associates. In each column (except the last one relating to imports), they show total dollars received in the five years 1985-89, divided by five. The last column shows the reduction in imports in billions of dollars.
[2]The peak in imports occured in 1981 for all countries except Brazil, where the peak was in 1980.

Source: Author's calculations based on sources in Table 2.2.

Table 5.1
Default Gains and Short-term Credits ($ bn)

	Maximum gain from default[1]	Outstanding short-term credits (1985)	Three months imports (1984)
Argentine	3.3	2.9	1.3
Brazil	8.8	3.4	3.9
Chile	0.9	1.4	3.9
Mexico	7.8	2.5	3.4
Venezuela	3.3	1.6	2.3
Philippines	-2.1	4.2	1.5

[1]See Table 3.6 for method of calculation.

Sources: Author's calculations based on materials cited in Table 3.6.

Table 6.1
Impact of Default on the U.S. Economy[1]
(Differences between default and base scenarios, percent)

	D.R.I. Simulation		Wharton Simulation	
Years after default[2]	1	2	1	2
GNP (cumulative effect)	-2.1	-3.2	-1.3	-0.9
Unemployment rate	+0.4	+1.0	+0.4	+0.6
Short-term interest rates	+1.5	-0.6	+2.3	0
Long-term interest rates	+0.5	0	+2.9	+1.8
Current Account ($bn)	-14	-48	-4	-2

[1]See text and Chapter 6, note 6 for explanation and analysis.

[2]Default occurs in January of year one; the figures in the table are the averages for that year and the following year.

Sources: Author's calculations based on Data Resources Inc., *U.S. Review,* September 1983 and Wharton Econometric Forecasting Associates, *What if Latin America Defaults?*

Table 6.2
Federal Reserve Response to Continental Illinois Crisis
(Reserves supplied before and after crisis, $m)

Make up day	Before Crisis (May 9th)	After Crisis (May 23)
Net borrowed reserves	417	3589[1]
Total bank borrowings	1063	4179[1]
Nonborrowed reserves	35151	32439[2]
Total reserves	36214	36619[3]

[1]The jump in these reserve measures reflects exceptionally heavy assistance to Continental Illinois through the discount window.

[2]The decline in this measure appears to reflect reserve draining to compensate for effects of discount window lending.

[3]The total reserve measure remained almost constant.

Source: James Capel & Co.

Table 6.3
Leading U.S. Banks' Exposure to Six Troubled Developing Countries[1]

Company	Mexico	Brazil	Venezuela	Argentina	Philippines	Chile	Six country total	Six-country total as % of shareholders equity[2]
BankAmerica	$2.7	$2.5	$1.5	$0.5	$0.3	$0.3	$7.8	150.9
Citicorp	2.9	4.8	1.4	1.2	1.7	0.5	12.5	206.7
Chase Manhattan	1.6	2.7	1.2	0.8	0.5	0.5	7.4	212.7
Manufacturers Hanover	1.9	2.2	1.1	1.3	0.4	0.7	7.8	268.5
Morgan	1.2	1.8	0.5	0.8	0.3	0.3	4.9	143.3
Continental Illinois	0.7	0.5	0.4	0.4	0.1	0.3	2.4	129.9
Chemical	1.4	1.3	0.8	0.4	0.4	0.4	4.6	196.7
Bankers Trust	1.3	0.7	0.4	0.3	0.2	0.3	3.3	177.6
First Chicago	0.8	0.7	0.2	0.2	0.2	0.2	2.4	126.9
First Interstate	0.7	0.5	0.1	0.1	0.1	0.1	1.5	70.8
Security Pacific	0.5	0.5	0.1	0.2	0.1	0.1	1.6	88.8
Wells Fargo	0.6	0.5	0.3	0.1	0.1	0.1	1.7	129.8
9 Money Centers	14.5	17.5	7.6	5.9	4.2	3.5	53.2	179.2

[1]Shown are cross-border risks, i.e., loans denominated in dollars. Exposures in most cases are from published company reports, or "ballpark" numbers based on conversations with bank managements. (Data are as of March 31, 1984.)

[2]Includes common and preferred.

Source: Becker Paribas Banking Industry Review, August 1984.

Table 6.4
Exposure of U.S. Banks to Third World Debtors

June 1984	209 Major Banks		Top 9 Banks		Next 15 Banks		Next 185 Banks	
	$ bn	Percent of Capital	$ bn	Percent of Capital	$ bn	Percent of Capital	$ bn	Percent of Capital
Mexico	25.8	30.4	14.3	41.9	5.1	33.0	6.4	18.2
Brazil	24.1	28.5	15.7	46.0	5.0	31.9	3.5	9.9
Korea	12.1	14.2	6.2	18.2	3.2	20.7	2.6	7.5
Venezuela	11.0	12.9	7.6	22.1	2.0	13.1	1.4	3.9
Argentina	8.7	10.3	5.7	16.6	1.9	12.4	1.4	3.9
Chile	6.3	7.5	3.6	10.5	1.3	8.0	1.5	4.1
Philippines	5.3	6.3	3.7	11.0	1.1	6.8	0.5	1.5
Colombia	3.3	4.0	2.3	6.9	0.6	3.3	0.5	1.4
Total	**96.6**	114.0	**59.1**	173.3	**20.2**	129.5	**17.8**	50.9
Total Capital	**84.7**		**34.1**		**15.6**		**35.0**	

Source: American Express Economics based on Federal Financial Institutions Examination Council, *Country Exposure Lending Survey*, June 1984.

Table 6.5
Earnings Reductions from Setting Up Loss Reserves
Reductions in earnings per share[1] from establishing loan loss reserve
on lending to six "problem" borrowers[2] of:

	1%	4%	6%	9%
BankAmerica	12	47	71	108
Citicorp	7	30	44	64
Chase Manhattan	10	39	59	89
Manufacturers Hanover	13	53	79	117
Morgan	6	23	35	46
Continental Illinois	11	45	67	100
Chemical	8	32	48	72
Bankers Trust	6	25	37	57
First Chicago	8	31	47	71
Average	9	36	54	81

[1]Based on actual 1983 earnings.

[2]These are the six countries in Table 6.3.

Source: George Salem, *Becker Paribas Banking Industry Review,* August 1984.

Table 6.6
Reducing Debt Exposure by Capitalization and Reserving
Exposure of the money center banks[1] to six problem borrowers,[2]
assuming interest capitalization of 5 percent annually

Loan Loss Reserves[3]	Bank equity growing at 5% annually			Bank equity growing at 10% annually		
	1984	1994	2004	1984	1994	2004
0	179[4]	179	179	179[4]	113	71
1	179[4]	162	148	179[4]	102	58
4	179[4]	121	82	179[4]	76	32
5	179[4]	110	66	179[4]	69	27

[1]Exposure as a percentage of shareholders' equity.

[2]Mexico, Brazil, Venezuela, Argentina, Philippines, Chile.

[3]Loss reserves established each year as percentage of outstanding loans to these countries.

[4]Actual exposure as percentage of equity in March 1984.

Source: Author's calculations.

Table 8.1
Restructuring or Default
($ bn annually, 1985–89)

	Total interest payments[1]		New Loans expected[2]		Temptation to default[3]	
	Currently	*After Re-structuring*	*Currently*	*After Re-structuring*	*Currently*	*After Re-structuring*
Argentina	6.5	5.1	1.2	1.6	3.3	1.5
Brazil	13.4	11.2	3.5	7.9	8.8	2.2
Chile	3.0	2.3	1.8	1.6	0.9	0.4
Mexico	13.0	10.0	4.2	7.1	7.8	2.0
Venezuela	4.4	3.9	0.5	2.7	3.3	0.5
Philippines	2.2	3.0	2.7	2.1	-2.1	-0.7

[1]Including interest of 5 percent capitalized annually (see text).

[2]Including capitalization of interest payments at 5 percent annually and new official lending (see text).

[3]See Table 3.6 and accompanying text.

Source: Author's calculations.